GW00419127

Speaking and Listening

Andrew Hammond

CONTENTS

How to use this pack 2

Planning for Speaking & Listening 3

IMAGES: Teacher's Notes and
Photocopymasters 1-20 4

SOUNDS: Teacher's Notes and
Photocopymasters 21-30 44

Cross-curricular links to QCA Schemes of Work 64

HOW TO USE MIND'S EYE SPEAKING and LISTENING

'Communication is crucial.'

'The ability to communicate is an essential life skill for all children and young people in the twenty-first century. It is at the core of all social interaction. With effective communication skills, children can engage and thrive. Without them, children will struggle to learn, achieve, make friends and interact with the world around them.'

These words are taken from the latest report on the Speech, Language and Communication needs of children and young people from 0-19 years. (The Bercow Report DCSF-00632-2008).

The Mind's Eye speaking and listening packs offer teachers exciting and engaging ways to develop the speaking and listening skills necessary for life and learning. As a parent of a five year old child said in the report: *"Speech, language and communication is the most important thing in all our children ... It's their key to life"*

Prepare

- Photocopy the student activity sheet (photocopymaster).
- Bring up the image and 'hide' using the hide and reveal tool on your interactive whiteboard.
- Read the teacher's notes.

Introduce the lesson

- Follow the step-by-step instructions at the top of the Teacher's Notes page. This will help to orientate the children to the image and support the later work.

Choose and deliver an activity/series of activities

- Choose either **Speaking**, **Listening**, **Group Discussion** or **Drama**.
- Follow the instructions for each activity or use them as a jumping off point for your own ideas for group work.
- Extend the students by using the Extension section at the bottom of the page.

Set a practice, assessment or homework piece of work

- Use the photocopymaster to lead this activity to elicit specific responses or to support planning and development of written and spoken English ideas.

PRIMARY NATIONAL STRATEGY FRAMEWORK FOR LITERACY
www.standards.dcsf.gov.uk/primaryframework/literacy

TEACHING OBJECTIVES COVERED IN MIND'S EYE YEAR 5

SPEAKING	• Tell a story using notes designed to cue techniques, such as repetition, recap and humour • Present a spoken argument, sequencing points logically, defending views with evidence and making use of persuasive language • Use and explore different question types and different ways words are used, including in formal and informal context
LISTENING	• Identify different question types and evaluate their impact on the audience • Identify some aspects of talk that vary between formal and informal occasions • Analyse the use of persuasive language
GROUP DISCUSSION	• Plan and manage a group task over time using different levels of planning • Understand different ways to take the lead and support others in groups • Understand the process of decision making
DRAMA	• Reflect on how working in role helps to explore complex issues • Perform a scripted scene making use of dramatic conventions • Use and recognise the impact of theatrical effects in drama

PLANNING FOR SPEAKING & LISTENING (YEAR 5)

In a useful handbook entitled *Speaking, Listening, Learning: working with children in Key Stages 1 and 2*, the DfES (2003) define the contexts, purposes and experiences needed for children to develop as effective speakers and learners in the following way:

Speaking: being able to speak clearly and to develop and sustain ideas in talk;

Listening: developing active listening strategies and critical skills of analysis;

Group discussion: taking different roles in groups, making a range of contributions and working collaboratively;

Drama: improvisation and working in role, scripting and performing, and responding to performances.

MAKING PROGRESS

Speaking
Can the pupils:
- organise and shape a talk, making connections between ideas and drawing on different points of view?
- use standard English appropriately?
- use persuasive techniques deliberately to influence the listener?
- use spoken language imaginatively, engaging the attention and interest of the listener?

Listening
Can the pupils:
- identify the importance of some key differences between formal and informal spoken language?
- analyse and evaluate how effectively speakers use language to argue and persuade?
- sustain listening to different sources, making their own notes?

Group discussion
Can the pupils:
- plan and manage work in groups with minimum supervision?
- understand and make use of a variety of ways to support, challenge and accept criticism?
- negotiate and make decisions taking account of alternatives and consequences?
- take different roles effectively, including leading the group?

Drama
Can the pupils:
- sustain and reflect on how different techniques for working in role help to explore complex issues?
- devise and perform a play for a specific audience?
- evaluate different aspects of a live performance, including characterisation, dramatic effects and suitability for different audiences?

ASSESSING AND RECORDING

To be able to trace pupils' progress effectively, follow these guidelines:

Make notes: much of the pupils' learning in speaking and listening takes place spontaneously, as comments are exchanged and ideas shared within paired and group discussions. Keep a 'talk diary' in which you can record notable comments made by pupils in the course of a Mind's Eye activity.

Take digital photographs: whenever possible, take digital photos of specific children involved in Mind's Eye activities. These could form a useful display to raise the status of speaking and listening activities in class.

Set goals: prior to a Mind's Eye activity, select specific targets drawn from the 'Making Progress' sections above and express them to the children, e.g. 'This time, let's focus on using gestures when we talk.'

Encourage self-evaluation: encourage the children to keep a record of their own progress in speaking and listening by evaluating their own performance in Mind's Eye activities, using a record sheet or 'talk diary' of their own.

Share successes: at the end of a particularly effective session, share ideas and elicit the children's own views about how they contributed and why the session was successful.

Record performances: using video cameras and/or audio equipment, record discussions and oral presentations. Play back and evaluate together.

Arrange 'assessed' activities: choose a specific Mind's Eye activity and explain to the class that it will be used as an assessment so they understand that for this particular activity you will be scoring the contributions made by each pupil. Plan to cover one activity from Speaking, Listening, Group Discussion and Drama over the course of the book (taken from a variety of different units).

TEACHER'S NOTES

Introduction

- Load up the Mind's Eye CD-ROM. You may like to tell the children what the title of the session is before you reveal the image, or just open up the picture and watch their initial reactions to it.

- With the whole image in view, revisit the children's first guesses and impressions. Establish what is happening: is this a silhouette/shadow of someone abseiling/climbing? Is the person wearing a backpack of some sort? Why?

Familiarisation

- Consider together how this image may have been created. Discuss how shadows are formed, etc.

- Elicit the children's prior knowledge and experience of climbing/abseiling. Why do people climb rocks? Do they enjoy the challenge?

Exploration

- Explore together any words and phrases to describe how the person in the image might be feeling, for eaxample, *nervous, excited, exhilarated, tired, anxious.*

- Encourage the children to think of other reasons why this person might be on a rope, for example, *being air lifted to safety, an SAS agent storming a building.*

Silhouette of person abseiling.
© Pixoi Ltd/Alamy

ACTIVITIES

Speaking

- **Talking partners:** Ask the children to imagine that the image they are seeing is the front cover of a story book. In pairs, the children make a list of good titles for this story, such as *To the Top, The Brave Climb, Rescued, Gravity.* Share these at the end and consider the kind of story plots these titles suggest.

- **Duologues:** In pairs, the children prepare, rehearse and perform short duologues involving two climbers. This could be the person in the picture and another holding the rope above. Focus particularly on the instructions and responses the climbers would say in this situation, i.e. *climb when ready, climbing, give me some slack,* etc. You might suggest that the climber/abseiler on the rope is actually afraid of heights, so will need some encouragement.

Listening

- **Reported conversations:** In pairs or small groups, the children consider the following question: *If you could climb up any natural or artificial structure, where would you climb, and why?* The children share responses and then, in a final plenary, report back on behalf of someone else.

👁 Group Discussion

- **Story narration:** As a whole class, or in groups, begin narrating a story about a challenging climb (possibly taken from one of the suggested titles and plots in the Speaking activity above). Each child contributes to the improvised story by adding a line of narration each time.

- **Group debate:** As a class, or in groups again, ask the children to consider the following motion: *Rock climbing is a dangerous pastime and should be banned. It is just not worth the risks.* Do the children agree? Are there ways of making rock climbing safe? Are we too obsessed with health and safety these days? Discuss together.

🎭 Drama

- **TV advertisement:** In pairs or small groups, the children prepare a short advertisement for television on behalf of a travel company that specialises in extreme activities for children, such as rock climbing, canoeing, surfing etc. Their task is to produce a one-minute presentation that is exciting, informative and very persuasive, to convince viewers to book a holiday with them.

❗ Extension

- **Scripted conversations:** In pairs, the children write a conversation, in playscript form, between a child and his/her parent in which the child tries to convince the parent to allow him/her to go on a rock-climbing course. The parent believes the child is too young for such dangerous activities and should wait another two years. Complete the storyline and perform to the class.

Name _____ Date _____

Look again at the image. See how the shadow allows us to work out what is going on.

Draw a shadow for some other extreme sports such as hang-gliding or bungee jumping and then see if your friends can guess what is going on. You will need to think about:

- the shapes the person will make during the activity
- any equipment you need to draw in.

Your friends may ask a maximum of ten questions to try to work out which sport you have drawn. You can only answer 'yes' or 'no' to their questions.

Extreme sport 1	Extreme sport 2

Extreme sport 3	Extreme sport 4

Don't forget to explain, in words, what is actually happening in each 'shadow scene' once your friends have had their guesses.

TEACHER'S NOTES

Introduction

- Load up the Mind's Eye CD-ROM. You may like to tell the children what the title of the session is before you reveal the image, or just open up the picture and watch their initial reactions to it.

- With the whole picture in view, share first impressions of the photograph: encourage the children to 'say what they see', listing features on the board, e.g. *monitors, control panels, a person, large windows, lights, aeroplanes* and so on.

Familiarisation

- Ask the children to share what they know about the term 'air traffic control'. Have they been to airports? Have they seen the control towers? What do they think happens in a room like this?

- Look closely at the image. Ask the children to list all the different colours they can see in it. *(Pink, blue, green, white, black, etc.)*

Exploration

- Consider what the atmosphere must be like in an air traffic control tower. Brainstorm key words and phrases to describe the mood of the place, for example: *stressful, pressurised, exciting, orderly, purposeful.*

- Look together at the person in the image. What do the children think he may be thinking/saying? Invite suggestions, and list them on the board.

Interior of air traffic control tower at LAX (Los Angeles, California) airport.
© Chad Slattery/Stone/Getty Images

ACTIVITIES

🗣 Speaking

- **Group brainstorms:** In cluster groups of about three or four, ask the children to brainstorm the sorts of skills and attributes they think a successful air traffic controller might need. After a few minutes, share ideas around the class, electing a spokesperson for each group.

- **Talking pairs:** In pairs, the children consider what the equipment in the image may be used for. Looking closely at the photograph, they discuss and make notes on the functions of some of the visible features in the room, such as *monitors, banks of switches, large screens* etc. Share ideas at the end.

👂 Listening

- **'Heathrow calling':** Find a wide open space – playground or school hall – and ask the children to get into groups of three or four. One group member acts as the air traffic controller; the other children are the aeroplanes. The task is to bring the planes in without colliding. You may wish to position the planes in a certain way, and then let them be guided in. There is one proviso: the 'planes' must have their eyes closed.

👁 Group Discussion

- **Class discussion:** Remind the children that computers play a vital role in air traffic control systems of today. Begin a class debate using the following motion: *This House believes that Man has become too reliant on computers.* The children must articulate their positions in response to the motion and listen very carefully to the opinions of others.

🎭 Drama

- **Duologues:** Divide the class into pairs. Each pair acts out a short conversation between an air traffic controller and the passenger of an aeroplane whose pilot has just suffered an injury. The controller must slowly and calmly guide the new 'pilot' through an emergency landing. The key thing here is not so much the terminology (which may prove elusive!) but the children's voice tones and expressions.

- **Group plays:** In larger groups, of six or seven, the children play out a scene from a giant control room at the Kennedy Space Centre. The actors sit in rows, simulating the banks of monitors. The key point in the drama is when we hear the message: *Houston, we have touched down on Mars!* How will they react?

❗ Extension

- **Diary:** In pairs, or individually, the children write an excerpt from an air traffic controller's diary, on the day 'we nearly lost a plane'. Encourage the children to share, and evaluate, each other's work.

Name _____   Date _____

THE NERVE CENTRE

Write a poem in which you describe the features and the atmosphere inside an air traffic control tower.

You will need to think about:

- the sights: flashing screens, lights, radar systems and switches
- the sounds: electronic beeps, radio communication and weather reports
- the staff: efficient, alert, expert.

Once you have written your poem in the space below, try to learn the words off by heart and perform it for the class.

TEACHER'S NOTES

Introduction

• Load up the Mind's Eye CD-ROM. You may like to tell the children what the title of the session is before you reveal the image, or just open up the picture and watch their initial reactions to it.

• With the whole image in view, share initial responses; brainstorm key words and phrases on the board, as they occur to the children, e.g. *moon, astronaut, NASA, lunar landing*.

Familiarisation

• Establish when and where this image may have been taken. Do they think this could be Neil Armstrong on the Moon, as he famously makes his 'one small step for man, one giant leap for mankind' speech?

• Elicit the children's prior knowledge of this famous lunar landing. Share information in class, recording any key dates and names on the board. Good examples are *Apollo 11, 1967, Neil Armstrong, Edwin (Buzz) Aldrin, Michael Collins, Sea of Tranquillity, NASA*.

Exploration

• Encourage the children to try to picture the scene and setting in their mind's eye. What is the astronaut looking at? Can the children describe the view, thinking about another astronaut taking the photograph, the lunar landscape, the spacecraft and the view of space beyond.

• Brainstorm key words and phrases in class to describe how the astronauts may be feeling at this time: *elated, relieved, privileged, nervous, overwhelmed*, etc.

Aldrin on the upper North surface of the Moon, 20th July 1969. Mirrored in his helmet are the moon-craft,'Eagle' and scientific instruments.
© akg-images

ACTIVITIES

Speaking

• **News report:** In pairs, the children take on the roles of newsreader and science correspondent to announce to the world the news that Apollo 11 has finally reached the Moon. The newsreader in the studio hands over to the correspondent who is outside Mission Control. Share role-plays in class.

• **Dialogue:** Ask the children to imagine they are the three astronauts involved in the lunar landing: Neil Armstrong, Edwin (Buzz) Aldrin and Michael Collins. Share feelings and responses as they touch down in the Sea of Tranquillity on the Moon. Share and evaluate conversations in class.

Listening

• **Children's news:** Discuss together how the news item performed in the Speaking session above might differ if it was written for a children's television channel. Discuss what the differences might be for a younger audience. What would be included or left out?

 Group Discussion

• **Planning committee:** In a circle, ask the children to imagine that the crew of the Apollo were unable to reach the Moon and were forced to turn back. Discuss together, in small groups, how, as the Public Relations Committee for NASA, you are going to break this bad news to the general public in a way that will not make them lose heart and believe it was a colossal waste of money (24 billion dollars).

Drama

• **Telephone calls:** In twos or threes, the children role-play two telephone conversations, both between an Apollo 11 crew member and his family. In the first he is just moments away from initial take off; in the second he has just returned to Earth after conquering the Moon. Share in class.

• **Hot-seating:** Invite volunteers to take the 'hot seat' and answer questions from the floor in the role of Aldrin, Armstrong or Collins. Can the children try to capture how these men must have felt? Encourage the class to ask sensible, thoughtful questions (and be sure to congratulate the astronauts at the end!).

Extension

• **Research and presentation:** Working individually, or in research pairs, the children find out more about the work of NASA. What does it stand for? What are its aims and objectives? The children may use a range of websites, CD-ROMs and library resources to find their information. They may even be able to retrieve some primary resource information from a relative! Share presentations in class.

Name _____   Date _____

THE FINAL FRONTIER

Can you imagine just how exciting the lunar landing must have been for people back on Earth? Ask your parents or grandparents to tell you how they felt watching these images on their TV screens.

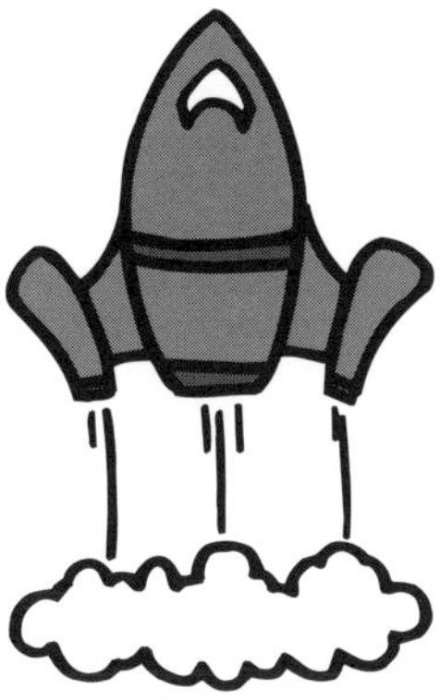

With a friend, discuss where you think Man will explore next, and when.

Make a list of the newly-discovered places you expect to see on your television screens in the future and guess when you think each place will be reached.

_____

_____

_____

_____

_____

_____

_____

_____

_____

_____

_____

_____

_____

TEACHER'S NOTES

Introduction

- Load up the Mind's Eye CD-ROM. You may like to tell the children what the title of the session is before you reveal the image, or just open up the picture and watch their initial reactions to it.

- With the whole picture in view, revisit the children's first impressions. Record key words and phrases on the board, e.g. *lights, Aurora, aliens, UFOs, starlight*.

Familiarisation

- Try to establish together where, and at what time of day, this photograph may have been taken. Look closely for clues from the house design, landscape, trees, weather, lights in the sky.

- Elicit what the children already know about the Aurora Borealis, a natural light show (known also as the Northern Lights), that can be seen in certain places near the North Pole. The light particles, known as 'solar wind', occur when particles from the Sun interact with the Earth's atmosphere.

Exploration

- Explore key words and phrases that capture the atmosphere of this place, such as *magical, mysterious, like a fantasy, in a dream, UFOs*.

- Consider what might be happening inside the house. Who is inside? What are they thinking / doing? Are they scientists studying the Aurora? Or are they new in town and fear the lights could be from aliens?

Aurora Borealis over home in Big Lake, Alaska, USA.
© *Stephen Nourse/Stone/Getty Images*

ACTIVITIES

🗣 Speaking

- **Duologue:** In pairs, the children pretend to be two people inside the house. One notices the lights outside and quickly tells the other. Together they discuss what this might be, sharing their thoughts and fears. Perform these conversations in class.

- **Hot-seating:** Invite volunteers to sit in the 'hot seat' at the front of the class and take questions from the floor, in the role of one of the people inside the house. Are they surprised by the lights outside their window? What did they think when they first saw them in the sky?

👂 Listening

- **Sound effects:** In pairs, or small groups, the children consider what sort of sound effects might accompany this image. They brainstorm these, trying out different sounds to explain what they mean, and listing them on a large sheet of paper. Share sounds in a final plenary, with the children focusing on the image as each group simulates their sounds. Which is the most exciting?

👁 Group Discussion

- **Class discussion:** The spectacular Aurora Borealis is a naturally occurring light show. Where and when else might we be equally amazed on this Earth? What other natural wonders can the children think of? Share ideas along the lines of *Niagara Falls, Grand Canyon, a starlit sky, a glacier or iceberg, a thick blanket of fog* and so on.

- **Committee:** Ask the children to imagine that the lights in the image are indeed from an extra-terrestrial force of some kind. In groups, the children form emergency committees to plan what they should do next on Earth. Who will they tell? Should they prepare to defend themselves? How can they give a message of peace to the visitors? Share views.

🎭 Drama

- **Television reporters:** In pairs, or larger groups, the children pretend to be a newsreader in a television studio and a roving reporter 'live at the light show'. The actors report the news of the strange lights appearing in the sky. The reporter might interview eye-witnesses – residents in the area – who first saw the lights emerging in the sky.

❗ Extension

- **Story:** Ask the children to draft, edit and read out an excerpt from an imaginary story about an alien landing. Their particular scene must describe 'the day I looked out of the window and saw a strange light...' Share and evaluate space story excerpts. Encourage the children to finish their stories. They may also be familiar with the Philip Pullman 'His Dark Materials' series, which includes the title 'Northern Lights', so may have ideas based on these texts.

Name _____   Date _____

AURORA BOREALIS

Did you know that the lights in the photograph occur naturally?
They are called the Aurora Borealis, or the Northern Lights.

Find out more about the Northern Lights. Look at websites,
CD-ROMs, books and magazines.

Prepare a short talk for your class, in which you (and a partner) amaze and
dazzle your friends with fascinating facts about this amazing light show at
the North Pole.

_____

_____

_____

_____

_____

_____

_____

_____

_____

_____

_____

TEACHER'S NOTES

Introduction

- Load up the Mind's Eye CD-ROM. You may like to tell the children what the title of the session is before you reveal the image, or just open up the picture and watch their initial reactions to it.

- With the whole picture in view, share first impressions of the photograph: record any key words and phrases on the board.

Familiarisation

- Look closely at the detail in the picture. Where could it have been taken? What could be happening here? Encourage the children to picture the wider context in their mind's eye and then describe it.

- Elicit the children's prior knowledge of mineshafts, caves and pot-holing etc. Record any known facts on the board.

Exploration

- Share key words and phrases to describe the scene from a sensory point of view, i.e. explore the sights, sounds, smells, touch and 'tastes' of the place. Make five columns on the board and list any key words.

- Explore the action in the scene. Is this a rescue operation? Is it a pot-holing team? Or is it a group of engineers working on London's drains? Create as many scenarios as you can together.

Caver in cave entrance, Yorkshire Dales, England.
© StockShot/Alamy

ACTIVITIES

Speaking

- **Paired work:** In pairs, the children list the different surfaces that can be seen in the photograph, such as rock, water, plastic (hat), glass (torch), cotton (man's overalls). Come together and share in a class plenary.

- **Dialogue:** What might this man, or woman, be saying? Could they be shouting to someone further up the tunnel? Or are they leading an expedition? In pairs, ask the children to explore possible lines and then share them in class. They will need to think carefully about the context, taking their cues from the detail in the picture.

Listening

- **Group talks:** In groups of about three or four, invite the children to share their views on pot-holing. Who would like to go exploring under the ground, and why? Encourage the children to listen carefully to each other's opinions and respond sensitively with relevant questions and comments.

Group Discussion

- **Class discussion:** Raise the subject of extreme sports, like pot-holing/ caving. Why do people do it? Can the children list a range of different extreme sports and then come up with some key words and phrases to sum up their appeal, i.e. *thrilling, for the challenge, exhilarating, something different, escapism*?

Drama

- **Group scenes:** Act out a scene in which a group of caving enthusiasts go exploring a new system of underground chambers and tunnels. One of their team becomes trapped/injured and they have to request special help to rescue them. The children play out the scene, focusing particularly on how they will use dialogue to comfort the injured/trapped member.

- **Adventure plays:** In similar groups, the children act out a scene in which a group of cavers are exploring underground when one of them disturbs something that is alive – perhaps a giant spider or man-eating mole, or even an alien that is colonising the Earth from beneath our feet! What will they do? Will they survive?

Extension

- **Research and presentation:** In pairs, or individually, the children find out more about caving, using a range of sources including the Internet, CD- ROMs, books and magazines. Start off the research with a question: *what is the difference between a cave and a pot-hole?* They could begin with the following useful websites: www.blackmountain.co.uk/land/cave.htm or www.vapours.force9.co.uk/main/caving/maincaving.html

Name _____ Date _____

THE OLD MINESHAFT

Write a play in which a group of children stumble across an old, disused mineshaft. Once inside, they discover a fascinating maze of tunnels and caves, but they soon become trapped. How will they get out?

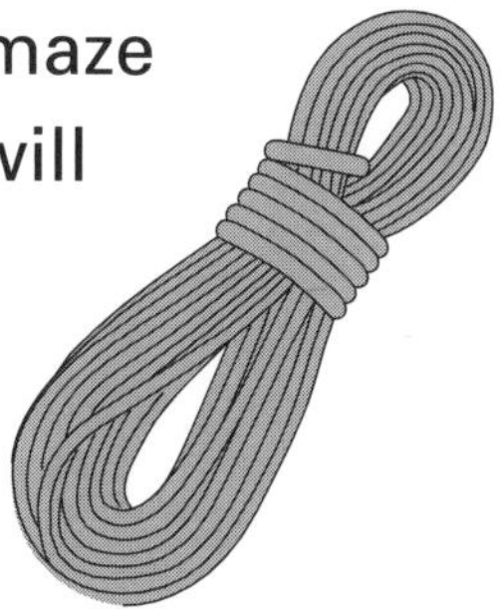

Begin drafting your play in the space below and then continue on another sheet. You will need to think about:

- the setting – use stage directions throughout
- the dialogue – keep it short and snappy – build excitement
- the plot – have a beginning, a crisis and then a dramatic rescue.

_____

_____

_____

_____

_____

_____

_____

_____

_____

_____

_____

In groups, work together to perform your play in class.

TEACHER'S NOTES

Introduction

- Load up the Mind's Eye CD-ROM. You may like to tell the children what the title of the session is before you reveal the image, or just open up the picture and watch their initial reactions to it.

- With the whole picture in view, revisit the children's first impressions and record any key words and phrases on the board, e.g. *chariot race, stallions, reins, Romans* etc.

Familiarisation

- Discuss when and where this photograph may have been taken. Look for clues to suggest the period, such as *modern fence, building at the end, telegraph poles in the distance, the fact that it is a photo.*

- Elicit the children's existing knowledge and experience of chariot racing: where and when have they seen it in action? Do we associate it with a particular country or period of history, such as the Romans?

Exploration

- Explore the atmosphere and excitement of a chariot race together. Record any key words and phrases to describe it, as the children imagine such a race in their mind's eye. Words and phrases could include: *clatter of hooves, cries from the riders, cheers from the crowd, trails of dust.*

- Look closely at the image and ask the children to see how many horses' hooves they can see. If this is indeed a race, how must the riders be feeling? Brainstorm key words and phrases to explore their thoughts, and fears as the race gets underway.

Photo from harness race held in Ogden, Utah, USA, where 20 million people watch harness racing events.
© Ted Wood/Stone/Getty Images

ACTIVITIES

 Speaking

- **Talking pairs:** Invite the children, in pairs, to make a list of modes of transport through the ages, including a pony and trap (a basic version of the chariot in the picture). Share lists in class. How many can they think of?

- **Word tennis:** Remind the children of the way we associate chariot racing with the Romans. But how well do they know their Romans? Invite two volunteers to take turns in sitting opposite one another at the front. The first player 'serves' by calling out any word of phrase associated with the Romans. The other player 'returns' with another and so on until someone falters. Try repeating this for the Greeks, The Tudors, Britain at War, and other history topics and themes.

Listening

- **Story narration:** In a class circle, or in smaller groups, the children improvise a collaborative story in which a chariot race takes place. As each child contributes to the narration, encourage them to use descriptive language to capture the atmosphere and set the scene.

Group Discussion

- **Class discussion:** In groups of three or four, the children consider how horses have been used over the years to help us in our daily lives. How has Man depended on 'horsepower' over the centuries? List the different ways together.

- **Class debate:** Consider together the question of whether horse racing is right. Do the horses enjoy it? Is it just for Man's pleasure? Thinking more generally, why should horses serve us in the way they do? How and when did we become their masters? Work through the questions together.

Drama

- **Role-play:** In twos or threes, the children prepare, rehearse and perform a short role-play in which a young Roman teenager battles with his/her parents to be allowed to enter his/her first chariot race. The child feels ready and able, but the parents think differently. Will the teenager win them over? He or she will have to be persuasive but polite! Listen to each other's negotiating skills.

Extension

- **Research and presentation:** Ask the children to find out more about chariot racing during Roman times or set them the more general task of considering what the Romans have done for us. How have our lives been made easier by the efforts of the Romans? Share findings in group discussions or presentations.

Name _____ Date _____

Design an eye-catching poster advertising the Annual Chariot Race.

You will need to think about:

- venue, times and cost of admission
- thrilling races taking place
- exciting displays and Roman re-enactments
- food and drink availability.

Design your poster in the space below, then use a larger sheet of paper to produce your best copy. Once you have finished the poster, present it to the class and talk about your design.

TEACHER'S NOTES

Introduction

- Load up the Mind's Eye CD-ROM. You may like to tell the children what the title of the session is before you reveal the image, or just open up the picture and watch their initial reactions to it.

- With the whole image in view, share first impressions of the picture, recording any key words the children volunteer on the board, e.g. *clocks, time, dials, faces, numbers, hands* and so on.

Familiarisation

- Invite the children to look closely at the image and find out: how many separate faces there are; what the different times are; how many of each number they can see.

- Revise how we measure time. Revisit the number of seconds in a minute, hour, day, and so on. How many minutes do they spend at school every day? How many seconds? (You may need to have a calculator handy!)

Exploration

- What do the children think this image may have come from? Could it be a piece of art, an album sleeve, a poster or a book cover? Where would they expect to see this kind of image around them?

- What does this image cause the children to see in their 'mind's eye'? How does it make them feel? Do they think of being late, timed exams, telling the time, mathematics? Share ideas on the board.

Yellow and blue clock faces representing overlapping time.
© Rob Bartee/Alamy

ACTIVITIES

🗣 Speaking

- **Talking partners:** Invite the children, in pairs, to list different ways in which time has been measured, and read, over the years. Share ideas in a final plenary: e.g. *sun dials, by the stars, tally charts, analogue, digital.*

- **Talking maths:** In pairs, ask the children to think of, and write down, a series of questions that they could ask others about a clock face. For example: *What is the total of all the numbers on a clock face when they are added together? What is opposite the 5 on a clock face? How many seconds does it take for the second hand to move from the 4 to the 9?* Share questions and quiz each other.

👂 Listening

- **Ticking clocks:** In a circle, invite the children to listen in silence to the clock on the wall ticking. Encourage them to become familiar with what a second 'feels like'. Then place the clock in a drawer and invite volunteers to estimate five seconds/twenty seconds/one minute and so on. (Time them using a 'silent' stop watch!). How close were they to the right amount of time?

👁 Group Discussion

- **Group discussion:** As a class, or in smaller groups, propose the question: *If this was the cover to a storybook, what might the story be about?* (Don't say time!) The children must think of brief story plots that suit such a book cover. Share story ideas at the end. These will be useful for the drama session below.

- **Class discussion:** As a whole class, consider the questions: *What would our lives be like if we didn't have to keep a track of time? Does time play too significant a role in our lives today?* Encourage the children to voice their own opinions and to listen attentively to the views of others.

🎭 Drama

- **Story narration:** In groups of five or six, or as a whole class, choose a story plot from the discussion above and begin improvising the story together, with each child contributing a line to progress the plot further.

❗ Extension

- **Research and presentation:** What is a cuckoo clock? Does it have a cuckoo inside? Where did the name come from? Why do we tend to associate clocks with Switzerland? Invite the children to conduct research to find answers to these questions. Encourage the children to present their findings at the end of the session.

Name _____ Date _____

IN THE YEAR 4005...

Think how much the process of telling the time has changed in the last two thousand years!

Now design a new type of watch for the year 4005. What will it look like? How big will it be? How will it work? Or will we all be fitted with timepieces in our heads so that we automatically know what the time is?

Sketch your design in the space below. Remember to include annotations (labels) to explain the features of your design.

Now see if you can present your idea to the class. You will need to talk about how, and why, you have chosen this particular design.

TEACHER'S NOTES

Introduction

- Load up the Mind's Eye CD-ROM. You may like to tell the children what the title of the session is before you reveal the image, or just open up the picture and watch their initial reactions to it.

- With the whole image in view, share first impressions of the scene, recording initial observations in the form of key words and phrases on the board, e.g. *pyramid, tour guide, hieroglyphics, tunnel, pharaoh* and so on.

Familiarisation

- Where do the children think this photograph may have been taken? Look closely at the detail in the image for clues: the patterns and paintings on the walls, the man's clothes, the light at the end, the surface of the floor. What else can they see?

- Elicit the children's existing knowledge of Ancient Egypt and its sites and treasures. Has anyone been to Egypt?

Exploration

- Encourage the children to picture the scene in their mind's eye. How do they feel as they walk down the long and narrow tunnel? Record responses on the board, using key adjectives and abstract nouns.

- Discuss where this walkway may lead and share ideas to assess which is the most likely. With each suggestion, encourage the child to describe what they see as they turn the corner at the end of the passageway.

Medinat Habu Temple of Ramses III, West Bank, Luxor, Egypt.
© Sindre Ellingsen/Alamy

ACTIVITIES

🗣 Speaking

- **Talking tour guides:** In pairs, the children exchange ideas about what this person might say as you approach him. Notice he has a hand out, in a beckoning manner. Is he a tour guide perhaps? After a few minutes, share lines of dialogue together. A good example is: *'This way to the pharaoh's tomb.'*

- **Group talk:** Divide the class into groups of about four. Each group discusses the question: *If this passageway could lead to wherever you wanted, where would it lead you, and why?* At the end, share views and opinions with the whole class, each child articulating their opinion clearly and listening attentively to the views of others.

👂 Listening

- **Walls in words:** Seat the class in a circle. Invite volunteers to imagine they are in the passageway in the image. They cannot see, and so they feel their way down the walls. Can they describe what they feel? Listen carefully and record any key words that help to convey the features and shape of the stones, such as *ridges, grooves, animal shapes, flat surfaces, indentations, lines.*

👁 Group Discussion

- **Group discussion:** Initiate a class discussion on the Pyramids of Ancient Egypt. What do we actually know about them? Why were they built? Why did they build them using this shape? What tools did they use? How did they move or lift the stones? Where could we look to find out this information? You may want to set this is a research project and come back together to discuss the findings the class has made.

🎭 Drama

- **Group scene:** In small groups, the children imagine they are visiting a pyramid in Egypt when suddenly the door closes and they are trapped inside. The scene must be a mime, so the children will need to convey what is happening through their facial expressions and body language.

- **Speaking hieroglyphics:** In small groups, decide on a phrase that sums up what could be buried in the Egyptian tunnels in the picture. Each person designs a hieroglyph to represent a word and then holds them up altogether to see if the rest of the group can identify what they have decided is hidden in the depths of the tomb!

❗ Extension

- **Group work:** In groups of about three or four, the children set about drafting, rehearsing and performing a short radio advertisement for holidays in Egypt. They will need to think about: the sights, accommodation, cuisine, flights and prices. If possible, record the adverts and play them back to the whole group.

Name _____ Date _____

Imagine you are a tour guide, like the figure in the photograph. You are standing at the entrance to a famous pyramid, welcoming in visitors and telling them about the surprises you have in store for them!

Write a few lines of dialogue in which you welcome the guests, tell them which way to go and explain what they will see as they journey deeper into the pyramid.

_____

_____

_____

_____

_____

_____

_____

_____

_____

_____

Now learn your words and perform your piece for the class. Imagine that the children watching you are tourists who have never been inside a pyramid before. Make sure you sound cheerful and enthusiastic!

TEACHER'S NOTES

Introduction

- Load up the Mind's Eye CD-ROM. You may like to tell the children what the title of the session is before you reveal the image, or just open up the picture and watch their initial reactions to it.

- With the whole picture in view, share first impressions of the scene, recording key words and phrases on the board, e.g. *wooden signpost, word 'help', clouds, sun, sky, dark silhouette.*

Familiarisation

- Look closely at the image: how many different colours can the children identify in the sky? Is this evening or morning? How can they tell?

- Elicit the children's existing knowledge and experience of signposts. What do they usually say? Share words and phrases on the board. Discuss the purpose of signposts generally: *to instruct, to direct, to highlight, to prohibit.*

Exploration

- Explore together where this signpost may be located. Share ideas on the board. Good examples are *heath land, mountainside, cliffs.*

- Discuss together reasons why the word 'help' might be written on the sign. Is it pointing heavenwards, perhaps? Has this image been digitally altered? Has the word *help* been superimposed onto the signpost?

Signpost pointing to 'Help'.
© Eyebyte/Alamy

ACTIVITIES

Speaking

- **Talking pairs:** Ask the children to work in pairs. Each pair must discuss, and make a list of, unusual words and phrases one might be surprised to see on a signpost and be pleased to be directed to! Some examples are: *sleep, sweets, happiness, peace and quiet.*

- **Guess the sign:** In small groups or pairs, children take turns to wear a sign on their forehead (a Post-It Note!) with the name of a place or building on it *(London, New York, castle, swimming pool)*. They cannot see the sign and must guess what it is by asking 20 questions, the answers to which may only be 'yes' or 'no'.

 Listening

- **Reported conversations:** In pairs, the children share their thoughts and experiences about times when they have had to ask for help. How did they feel? Did they get the help they needed? At the end, invite the children to share their stories, speaking on behalf of their partners, or for themselves. Examples may include: *asking difficult questions in class, directions in a new school, carrying something* etc.

 Group Discussion

- **Class discussion:** Initiate a discussion on ways in which the children help their parents at home. List the different ways on the board. Some starting points are: *tidying up, washing the car, washing up, breakfast in bed, behaving well!* How many does each child do and could they improve on this?

- **Group discussion:** Look again at the image of the 'help' sign. Introduce the idea that this could be a metaphor for the times in our lives when we may need some direction or guidance. Who helps us in our lives? Who do we turn to when we feel lost *(parents, grandparents, teachers, our religion, friends)*?

Drama

- **Group play:** In small groups, or in pairs, the children prepare, rehearse and perform a short sketch in which they find themselves lost in a remote place and are in need of help. They stumble across this sign and follow it, but is it real, or is it a hoax? What kind of help do they need? Share and evaluate the scenes.

Extension

- **Signs galore:** Invite the children to pay attention to the signs that they pass on their journeys to school and record the words and phrases they see in a notebook. Encourage them to group the signs into different categories, such as directions, warnings, guidance, names and instructions. The children present their findings to the class. You may wish to make a class display!

Name _____ Date _____

Everybody needs help sometimes. Think carefully about the ways in which you can help your friends when you are at school. It may be in the classroom, on the sports field or in the playground.

Write down 10 ways in which you can help each other and make your school a happier place!

For example:

- cheer up a friend if they're looking glum
- help a new pupil find new friends
- listen to others' ideas without interrupting!

HELPING AT SCHOOL:

1 _____

2 _____

3 _____

4 _____

5 _____

6 _____

7 _____

8 _____

9 _____

10 _____

Now see if you can write down 10 different ways of helping at home.

Keep this guide handy, so that you can remind yourself how to be a helpful, happier pupil! Just think – the person your friends will be helping is YOU!

TEACHER'S NOTES

Introduction

- Load up the Mind's Eye CD-ROM. You may like to tell the children what the title of the session is before you reveal the image, or just open up the picture and watch their initial reactions to it.

- With the whole image in view, encourage the children to share their first impressions, brainstorming any key words and phrases that come into their heads as they look at the picture, e.g. *London Eye, London, city, views, pods, capsules, Ferris wheel* etc.

Familiarisation

- Establish that this is the London Eye. Ask when it was built, and why, where it is located, and why it has been so popular. Has anyone been on the wheel? What was it like?

- Elicit the children's knowledge and experience of Ferris wheels. Where are they usually found? How do they work? What makes this one so unique?

Exploration

- Encourage the children to try to imagine they are inside one of the pods. What do they see in their mind's eye? Invite them to use words and phrases to describe the view across London.

- Explore together adjectives and abstract nouns that accurately capture how one might feel riding the wheel, such as: *excited, impressed, frightened, anxious, thrilled, fear, vertigo* and so on.

The London Eye at night, London SE1.
© ACE STOCK LIMITED/Alamy

ACTIVITIES

Speaking

- **Advertisements:** In pairs, the children prepare, rehearse and perform a few lines of speech in which they advertise the London Eye to the pedestrians who are walking past it. For example: *roll up, roll up, see the greatest city in the world from inside a space capsule! Come float on the breeze above the rooftops!*

- **Hot-seating:** Invite volunteers to sit in the 'hot seat' (a free chair) at the front of the class, and answer questions from the others in the role of someone who has been on the London Eye. (If any children have been begin with them!)

Listening

- **Circle games:** Seat the class in a circle around you. Explain that you are going to play a memory game in which each child recites the line: *When I was up in the sky on the London Eye I spied... .* The children must add a building, London landmark or common feature of a city to the list, but must recite all those that have gone before first!

Group Discussion

- **Class discussion:** Find pictures of the London Eye to show to the class. Then ask the questions: *Why was it built? What does it do for London? Does it fit in? Is it supposed to be a bold statement to say that London is a modern, exciting city?* What do the children think?

Drama

- **Group role-play:** In groups of about three of four, the children prepare, rehearse and perform a scene together in which they are sharing a pod on the London Eye. One of the party suffers from vertigo and becomes very nervous and uncomfortable as the pod climbs higher. How will they calm him/her down?

- **Presentation:** Imagine the London Eye has not yet been built. In pairs or groups of three, the children prepare a short presentation to give to a London planning committee (the rest of the class) persuading them that the London Eye would be good for London and should be built next to the River Thames.

Extension

- **Letter of complaint:** Working individually, the children imagine they are a resident/office worker in a building close to the site for the London Eye. Write a letter of complaint to the Greater London Authority/City Council, objecting strongly to the proposed plan to construct a giant Ferris wheel outside their window! The children read, and evaluate, their letters.

Name _____ Date _____

MORE RIDES FOR LONDON

What else could be built on the banks of the River Thames to attract more tourists? A ghost train? Giant dodgem cars?

Prepare a short presentation to give to a planning committee outlining your plan for a new and exciting ride across the river from the London Eye.

You will need to think about:

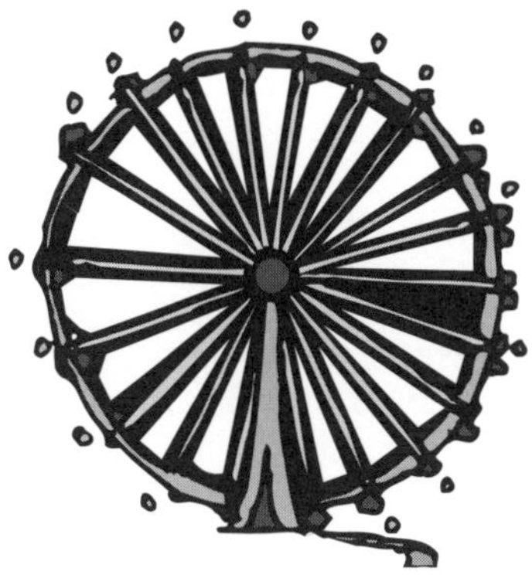

- what the ride will look like
- how long it will take to build
- how much it will cost
- why people will like it
- what it will do for London.

Write some notes to help you when you give your presentation.

_____

_____

_____

_____

_____

_____

_____

_____

_____

TEACHER'S NOTES

Introduction

- Load up the Mind's Eye CD-ROM. You may like to tell the children what the title of the session is before you reveal the image, or just open up the picture and watch their initial reactions to it.

- With the whole image in view, share initial responses; brainstorm key words and phrases on the board, as the children are encouraged to 'say what they see'.

Familiarisation

- Elicit the children's prior knowledge of the Incas and Machu Picchu itself. Have they ever seen anything like this before? Where do they think this may be located in the world? How old might these ruins be?

- Establish that 'Machu Picchu' means 'old mountain' in Quechua, the ancient language of the Incas, in Peru. This citadel was built as a centre of worship and astronomic observatory for the Incas and their ruler, Pachacutec.

Exploration

- Encourage the children to try to picture the great citadel in its heyday. Can they describe, using their mind's eye? Record key words and phrases on the board, e.g. *grand, spectacular setting, religious, arches and pillars, whole community in the clouds,* etc.

- Invite the children to suggest words and phrases that describe the site as they see it now, such as *mysterious, ancient, ruins, archaeological importance, Peru's treasure.*

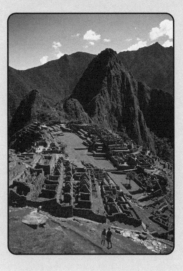

Machu Picchu, Peru.
© Jon Arnold Images/Alamy

ACTIVITIES

🗣 Speaking

- **Duologue:** In pairs (preferably boy/girl) the children imagine they are the two people in the foreground, visiting the site for the first time. Encourage them to share their reactions to the place in a conversation that can then be performed to the rest of the class.

- **Exchanging views:** In small groups or pairs, the children exchange their views on where in the world they might travel for a holiday if they were interested in ancient sites like the one in the image. They will need to compile a short list of these and then present them back to the class. Venues might include: *Pyramids in Egypt, temples in China, monasteries in Nepal, Stonehenge/abbeys in England.*

👂 Listening

- **Narrated story:** In a large circle, or in smaller groups, the children improvise a collaborative story together, each one listening carefully and contributing a line of narration as the story is 'passed' around the group. The theme must be 'the lost city in the mountains'.

👁 Group Discussion

- **Class discussion:** Initiate a discussion on what life might have been like for the Incas at Machu Picchu. Share views and theories about a day in the life of an Inca long ago. Think about the location in the mountains, the weather, the natural resources available and so on.

- **Group discussion:** In small groups, the children discuss and compile a list of ideal questions that will guide future research into the Incas. Once they have made a list of about 10, share these in a class plenary. Questions could include: *How old is this site? Who were the Incas? How did they live? When did they leave this place? Are there other sites like it in Peru/around the world?*

🎭 Drama

- **Telephone calls:** In twos, the children enact a short telephone sketch in which one person plays the part of a travel agent, the other a customer, looking for an adventurous holiday. The travel agent begins with the line: *Have you thought of Inca trekking in Peru?* The customer asks a series of questions which the travel agent must answer.

🔴 Extension

- **Television advertisement:** In small groups, or pairs, the children imagine they are working for the Tourist Board of Peru. Their task is to write and perform a short advertisement for British television in which they sell the idea of coming to Peru for 'the holiday of a lifetime'. Share in class.

Name _____   Date _____

INCA FACTFILE

Work with a partner and conduct some research on the Incas, using the questions you devised earlier. You may be able to use the Internet, CD-ROMs, encyclopaedias and brochures to locate your information.

You will need to think about:

- when the Incas were around
- how they lived
- what they built together
- how they came to be in Peru.

PERU

Record any information you find in the space below, then put together a short presentation for your class.

_____

_____

_____

_____

_____

_____

_____

_____

_____

_____

TEACHER'S NOTES

Introduction

- Load up the Mind's Eye CD-ROM. You may like to tell the children what the title of the session is before you reveal the image, or just open up the picture and watch their initial reactions to it.

- With the whole picture in view, share first impressions of the scene, recording key words and phrases on the board, i.e. the first words that come into the children's minds.

Familiarisation

- Consider together what sort of ape this is. Establish that it is an orang-utan. Consider where, when and why this photograph may have been taken.

- Elicit the children's existing knowledge and experience of apes, their needs and their habits. Do they suit being in captivity? Has anyone seen an orang-utan? Can they describe it? Does anyone know what the word 'orangutan' actually means? (Man of the forest.)

Exploration

- Look closely at the image. Focus on the orang-utan's face and eyes. Brainstorm together what (s)he might be thinking. Encourage the children to describe the facial expression and the thoughts that may lie behind it.

- Establish that this is quite a powerful image. What does it say to the children? Encourage them to articulate their thoughts and responses.

Orang-utan (Pongo Pygmaeus) at Hong Kong's Zoological and Botanical Gardens.
© John Hay/Lonely Planet Images/Getty Images

ACTIVITIES

Speaking

- **Striking contrasts:** In pairs, the children make a list of contrasting adjectives to illustrate the difference between this animal's native habitat and the location in which he now finds himself. For example; *colourful, lush, soft, verdant, fertile, free* versus *hard, metallic, austere, dull.* Share and evaluate these in class.

- **Talking captions:** In pairs or small groups, the children list five captions that could accompany this image, perhaps for a magazine or poster. Share these in class.

Listening

- **Circle/memory game:** In a circle, begin a memory game in which each pupil must take turns in reciting the following line: *On my rainforest holiday I saw... .* The children must add their own creature at the end of the line, after reciting all those that have gone before. This can be extended by asking the children to give each creature an actual name as well, i.e: a firefly called Fred, a tree frog called Trevor, and so on.

 Group Discussion

- **Class debate:** Consider the following motion, encouraging children to write speeches in support or opposition to it: *This House believes that animals should not be kept in captivity.* Children share views, listening and responding sensitively to others' opinions. Remind them of the benefits of zoos as well as the problems, considering the pros and cons of breeding programmes, education, research and development.

Drama

- **Duologues:** In pairs, the children role-play a conversation in which one person likes visiting zoos and the other believes that animals should not be kept in captivity at all. Focus on how their opposing views can be reconciled. Encourage the pairs to perform for the class and evaluate performances.

- **Movement and sound:** Consider together: how does an orang-utan move? What sort of sounds does (s)he make? In a large space, invite the children to emulate the sounds and movement of apes. Have fun! Find out who is the most ape-like in the class! You may be able to show footage of real apes.

Extension

- **Research and presentation:** In pairs, or individually, the children find out more about orang-utans. They may use the Internet, CD-ROMs, encyclopaedias and magazines. The following websites are excellent sources: www.orangutan.org.uk and www.orangutans-sos.org

Name _____   Date _____

Did you know that orang-utans are in grave danger of becoming extinct because their natural habitat – the rainforest – is disappearing around the world?

Find out more about this beautiful, but endangered animal and design a persuasive poster that informs people about the plight of the orang-utans. It should also tell them how they can help to save these creatures from extinction.

Draw a first draft of your poster below, and then design a proper version on a large sheet of paper.

TEACHER'S NOTES

Introduction

- Load up the Mind's Eye CD-ROM. You may like to tell the children what the title of the session is before you reveal the image, or just open up the picture and watch their initial reactions to it.

- With the whole image in view, elicit the children's first impressions, recording their words on a mind-map on the board. These may be restricted to adjectives, or can be any words and phrases they think of when they look at the picture.

Familiarisation

- Ask the children to consider: how many skydivers there are; how far up they may be; what is on the ground below them; how far away is the plane; what is the weather like; why are they linking arms?

- Invite the children to think about why, when and where this is taking place. Is it a special event? Could it be a sponsored jump or perhaps a record-breaking attempt?

Exploration

- Ask the children to view the image in a more imaginative way by describing what they see in metaphors, similes and symbols. For example: *a rainbow of divers, confetti in a breeze, the spokes of a wheel, a human patchwork, falling starfish.*

- Ask the children to sum up the image in a single word – any word – that captures the mood of the picture. Ideas might include: *freedom, courage, friends, life, freefall.*

Formation skydiving in action.
© Buzz Pictures/Alamy

ACTIVITIES

Speaking

- **Talking partners:** Working in pairs, ask the children to role-play a scene in which two skydivers are sitting on the plane, moments before the jump, sharing their thoughts. One has jumped many times before, the other is a beginner.

- **Formation fun:** Working in pairs or individually, the children have one minute to list as many sports or activities as they can that might be performed in formation, like the skydiving in the picture. After one minute, see who has the most suggestions and hear the lists read aloud.

Listening

- **Memory game:** Seat the class in a large circle. Ask the children to pretend that everyone is into extreme sports. Invite the children to take turns in saying: *When we're not at school we like to go...* (insert an extreme sport). Each time a person speaks, (s)he must recall the previous sports and then add a new one!

- **Telephone conversation:** In pairs, the children sit back-to-back (so they cannot see each other), and perform a telephone dialogue in which a skydiver describes the experience of jumping to a friend who missed the event.

Group Discussion

- **Debate:** Hold a group discussion in which the following motion is debated: *This House believes that extreme sports should be left to the professionals; skydiving is not for amateurs.* Have two proposers, two opposers and questions from the floor (see activity sheet).

Drama

- **Group Geronimo!:** Create a large space in the centre of the room and ask the children to link arms together, simulating the pattern in the picture. On the count of three, the jump will begin. Ask the children to simulate falling (for a few seconds), with facial expressions, body language and cries to match. At a given moment, shout freeze and observe/appraise everyone.

- **Group scene:** Divide the children into small groups. Ask each group to role-play a scene in which they are gathered around a television set, watching a training video on the morning of the jump. None of them have jumped before and parts of the video frighten some viewers! Will they still go ahead?

Extension

- Invite the children to form writing partnerships in which they write a short playscript involving a record-breaking skydive that nearly turns to disaster when the weather becomes stormy. There are no fatalities, but the skydivers are shaken. How will they cope with the weather and their nerves?

Name _____ Date _____

'LIVE AT THE SCENE...' ⓐⒷⒸ

A television reporter is live at the scene of the world's largest formation skydiving attempt.

Use the space below to prepare a range of questions for the reporter to ask the brave skydivers as they descend from the skies.

1 _____

_____

2 _____

_____

3 _____

_____

Now work with a partner to rehearse and perform a pretend interview in which these, and other, questions are asked.

WHAT DO YOU THINK?

The class is about to debate the following motion:

This House believes that extreme sports should be left to the professionals; skydiving is not for amateurs.

Can you think of some points for and against the motion?

For	Against
1 _____	1 _____
_____	_____
2 _____	2 _____
_____	_____

TEACHER'S NOTES

Introduction

• Load up the Mind's Eye CD-ROM. You may like to tell the children what the title of the session is before you reveal the image, or just open up the picture and watch their initial reactions to it.

• With the whole image in view, share first impressions of the image. Brainstorm key words on the board as the children 'say what they see'.

Familiarisation

• Elicit the children's prior knowledge of the International Space Station (ISS). Have they seen pictures of it before? What do they think of it? Where is it located? What is it for? How do they think this image was taken?

• Discuss this view of Earth together. What makes up the colours in the image? What percentage of the planet is water/land?

Exploration

• Explore together how it must feel to be on board the ISS. Share words and phrases, e.g. *exciting, exhilarating, hard work, nerve-wracking, tense, magical* and so on.

• What is the blackness of space? Can the children picture the ISS in their mind's eye and then describe the surrounding views?

Satellite view of Mir Space Station orbiting over Earth in 1995, photographed from the US Space Shuttle Atlantis.
© NASA/Getty Images

ACTIVITIES

Speaking

• **Talking partners:** Ask the children to work in pairs. Each pair must make a list of interesting adjectives and adjectival phrases to describe this view of Earth. Good examples are: *iridescent jewel, blue stone, magical seas, precious planet, blue paradise.*

• **Group brainstorm:** In groups of about three of four, the children brainstorm compound words that begin with the word 'space–', e.g. *spacesuit, spaceship, spaceman.* How many can the children think of? Share at the end.

Listening

• **Reported conversations:** Would the children like to travel in space? How would they feel? Would they like to become an astronaut? In pairs, they exchange views in response to these questions. Then, in a final plenary, invite the children to feedback to the group, speaking on behalf of their partners.

Group Discussion

• **Group debate:** As a class, debate the following motion: *'This House believes that the millions of dollars spent on space exploration should be put towards relieving world famine. We should feed the starving people of this planet before seeking out new ones.'*

Drama

• **Duologues:** In pairs, the children take on the roles of two astronauts preparing for a mission to the ISS. One astronaut has been several times before, while for the other this is a debut voyage. The characters share thoughts, fears and hopes. Invite volunteers to share their performances in class at the end.

• **Group drama:** In groups of about three of four, the children imagine they are on board the ISS. The scene they must act out is 'the day they saw a UFO through the porthole'. Share performances at the end. Encourage the children to focus on their facial expressions as well as their dialogue when the UFO first appears.

Extension

• **News report:** In pairs, the children write, rehearse and perform a short report for a television news programme, in which the completion of the ISS is announced. The project is now finished and astronauts can begin using the ISS as a home for research. Have one anchor man/woman in the studio and a roving reporter outside the USA's Kennedy Space Centre/Gagarin Centre in Russia.

Name _____ Date _____

'HOUSTON, WE HAVE A PROBLEM...'

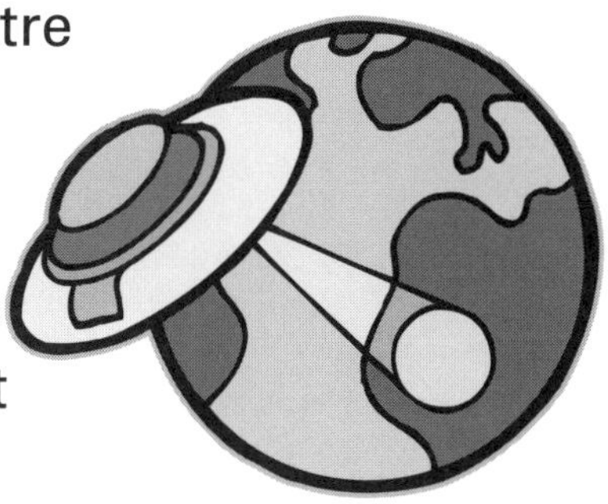

Imagine you are on board the International Space Centre (ISS). Suddenly, you pick up a strange object on your radar screen, signalling that something, or someone, is approaching the ISS!

You must report to space headquarters on Earth. What will you say? How will the controllers on Earth react?

Write the conversation that you might have with mission control.

Astronaut: _____

_____

Control: _____

_____

Astronaut: _____

_____

Control: _____

_____

Astronaut: _____

_____

Control: _____

_____

Rehearse your conversation and then perform it for the class. Remember to make it sound exciting and full of suspense: after all, it's not every day that we see an alien spaceship!

TEACHER'S NOTES

Introduction

• Load up the Mind's Eye CD-ROM. You may like to tell the children what the title of the session is before you reveal the image, or just open up the picture.

• With the whole picture in view, share first impressions of the scene, recording key words to describe what the pupils see in the picture, mentioning visible features only to begin with, e.g. *large house, gardens, woods, long grass, clouds* etc.

Familiarisation

• Look closely at the image. Invite the children to suggest where and when this photograph may have been taken. Look closely together for clues in the picture, such as the design of house, materials used to build it, sky, land use, type of trees etc.

• Elicit the children's existing knowledge and experience of large stately homes like this one. Have they ever visited somewhere like it? Was it privately owned or run by the National Trust perhaps? Were they impressed?

Exploration

• Brainstorm key words and phrases that can be used to describe the atmosphere and mood of this image. Would it make a difference if the photograph was in colour? Does the sky make a difference; would it feel different if the sky was bright and cloudless?

• Explore together who might live in a house like this. Encourage volunteers to share their original ideas, such as *a family of vampires, an old eccentric magician, two elderly spinsters*.

Woodlawn House, County Galway, Ireland.
© The Marsden Archive/Alamy

ACTIVITIES

Speaking

• **Brainstorming partners:** In pairs, the children imagine that this house has been neglected for many years. They make a list of words and phrases to describe the interior of the house, its features and atmosphere, e.g. *cracked window panes, moth-eaten curtains, a carpet of cobwebs, scurrying rats, moonlit spiral stairs.*

• **Word tennis:** Ask for two volunteers to sit opposite one another at the front of the class and play a game in which one player 'serves' by calling out one feature they can see in the image, such as *cloud, grass, window, chimney, bricks, porch*. The other player 'returns' with a different feature, and so on until someone loses a point through hesitation or repetition.

Listening

• **Reported conversations:** In pairs, the children exchange views in answer to the following question: *If you could live in any type of house at all, what would it be like?* After about 10 minutes, form a circle and share views, with each child speaking on behalf of their partner.

Group Discussion

• **Class discussion:** Consider the question: *How have houses in this country changed over the centuries?* Encourage the children to pool their knowledge about house design over the years. You may wish to record on the board the different building materials that have become available over time, starting with *wood, straw, wattle and daub, bricks, cement, steel, glass, concrete* and so on.

• **Group talks:** In small groups, the children narrate an improvised story that involves a haunted house, like the one in the picture. Each child contributes a line of story narration as the story is 'passed around' the group circle. Stop and listen to each group's story after a while.

Drama

• **Group play:** In small groups, the children prepare, rehearse and perform a short scene in which a number of them pretend they are entering an old, derelict house. The actors mime, as other members of the group add different sound effects, to which the actors must react via their facial expressions and body language, e.g. *door slams, floorboards creak, wind howls, someone laughs.*

Extension

• **House particulars:** In pairs, or individually, the children prepare house particulars for this house, pretending it is on the market and they are the sole agents! They will need to focus on the interior/exterior, land, location, price, etc. You may like to download a few details from some local property websites or local newspapers to give examples of the type of language and format they should consider.

Name _____ Date _____

THE HARD SELL

Imagine you are trying to sell the house in the picture and you think you may have found a buyer. Try to persuade this person that they need to pay a visit to the house immediately.

Be persuasive and list all the wonderful features this house has to offer, but remember, the caller may be quite fussy and may ask lots of difficult questions!

Write a transcript of the telephone conversation below.

Agent: _____

_____

Caller: _____

_____

Agent: _____

_____

Caller: _____

_____

Agent: _____

_____

Caller: _____

_____

Agent: _____

Find a partner and read through your script together, then perform it for your class. Who is the most persuasive agent and the fussiest customer?

TEACHER'S NOTES

Introduction

- Load up the Mind's Eye CD-ROM. You may like to tell the children what the title of the session is before you reveal the image, or just open up the picture and watch their initial reactions to it.

- With the whole image in view, share first impressions of the scene, encouraging the children to 'say what they see' to begin with.

Familiarisation

- Consider together where this place might be. What is happening in the scene? When might this have been taken? Share initial reactions and theories. Do any of them have relatives who lived through the Blitz and who have discussed this time with them?

- Establish that this is a view of St Paul's Cathedral during the London Blitz in the Second World War. Elicit the children's prior knowledge of this period of history, focusing specifically on conditions in London during the raids. Brainstorm key words and phrases associated with this period, e.g. *Homefront, Blitz, air raid sirens.*

Exploration

- Brainstorm key words and phrases that capture how it might have felt to be caught up in the Blitz, for example: *overwhelming, frightening, confusing, suffocating.*

- Then explore together words and phrases that accurately sum up the British spirit during the war. Good examples include: *courageous, stoical, pulling together, helping each other, resilient* and so on.

View over London around St Paul's Cathedral during World War II bombings, 29th December 1940.
© akg-images

ACTIVITIES

 Speaking

- **New report:** Invite the children to work in pairs. Their task is to prepare a short radio news report the morning after a particularly ferocious air raid on the St Paul's area of London. One person may be the newsreader, the other a roving reporter out in the field. If the children work in larger groups, they may include eyewitness accounts. Remember to focus on the need to report the events, but to keep the public's spirits up (you may wish to discuss the idea of propaganda).

- **Talking captions:** In small groups the children come up with suitable captions that might accompany this image, were it to appear in a London newspaper the next day. Share and evaluate work.

 Listening

- **Circle game:** Explain that St Paul's is a very famous landmark in this country. Can the children think of any other famous landmarks? Share ideas in a circle, each person listening carefully to others' ideas (and avoiding repetition).

 Group Discussion

- **Class discussion:** Introduce/revisit the word *Evacuation* in a class discussion. Elicit the children's knowledge of it, and their reactions too: would they like to have been evacuated? Share opinions together. Ask the children to make notes throughout the discussion about how and why evacuees were sent into the countryside during the war.

- **Group discussion:** In groups, the children consider the following questions: *Can war be justified? Is there a better way of solving conflicts? How do wars begin? How can they be avoided?* Each group makes notes and presents their views to the class in a final plenary.

Drama

- **Hot-seating:** Invite volunteers to take the 'hot seat' at the front of the class and answer questions from the floor in the role of a London resident caught up in the Blitz. Encourage the questioners to find out about this person's experiences, hopes and fears for the future. (The year is 1940.)

Extension

- **Group role-play:** Divide the class into groups of about four. Each group writes, rehearses and performs a short sketch in which a London family wake up the morning after an air raid, to find their street unrecognisable. How will they react, as they venture outside and see the devastation? Will they feel defeated, or will their resolve be strengthened further?

Name _____ Date _____

THE BLITZ

Look again at the image of St Paul's Cathedral under fire in the London Blitz.

Write a poem using interesting words and phrases to capture the atmosphere of the place, and the courage of the people. You may like to think about:

- the sounds of the air raid sirens and the planes overhead
- the sight of the flames and the people running for cover
- the smell of smoke and dust
- the feel of rubble and splintered wood beneath your feet.

Draft your poem in rough first, then write it out neatly in the space below. You could include illustrations too.

TEACHER'S NOTES

Introduction

• Load up the Mind's Eye CD-ROM. You may like to tell the children what the title of the session is before you reveal the image, or just open up the picture and watch their initial reactions to it.

• With the whole image in view, share initial responses; brainstorm key words and phrases on the board, as the children 'say what they see'.

Familiarisation

• Look closely at the image: what has happened here? How did the ship sink? Where is it set? Is this a famous ship? How many lifeboats can the children count?

• Introduce and discuss the famous ship, the Titanic. Is this it? How can we tell? Elicit the children's existing knowledge of the Titanic's extraordinary history. Share information and record key facts and events on the board. (Bear in mind that much of the class's references could come from the film, *Titanic*.)

Exploration

• Encourage the children to see the scene in their mind's eye. Invite volunteers to describe the atmosphere and setting. Record key words and phrases on the board, e.g. *icy cold, emergency, helpless, panic-stricken.*

• Explore together captions that might accompany this image were it to appear in a magazine or newspaper. What would be a powerful headline for this story? Some examples are: *Maiden voyage turns to disaster, Titanic No More, Thousands perish in icy seas.*

Photograph coloured in the style of a watercolour showing the sinking of the Titanic, 14th April 1912.
© akg-images

ACTIVITIES

Speaking

• **Dialogue:** Ask the children, in small groups, to imagine they are among the survivors in a lifeboat. Share dialogue in character about their feelings in response to the disaster, their grief and their hopes about getting home. Share and evaluate performances in class.

• **Hot-seating:** Take turns to sit in the 'hot seat' at the front of the class and answer questions in character as: the ship's designer, captain, owner or crew member. Encourage the children to ask thoughtful and searching questions about who was to blame, what was done to avoid the disaster and how they coped.

Listening

• **Port/starboard:** In a large space (hall/playground), play a listening game. The children run around independently until you shout a series of different calls, each one requiring them to stay motionless in particular positions or places. Use the terms: *port (left), starboard (right), bow, stern, captain's coming, climb the rigging, man the lifeboats, scrub the decks.* The last person to follow your instructions sits out each time.

Group Discussion

• **Class discussion:** In a circle, consider together how the general public must have felt when the Titanic was first launched. What might their first impressions have been? Would they have thought it was the grandest ship on Earth/too big/it'll never float/the most luxurious thing ever seen/just for the rich, not for me. Compare this to how they must have greeted the news of it sinking.

Drama

• **News report:** Working individually or in pairs, the children plan, draft and perform a short radio announcement in which news of the Titanic disaster is first announced to the listening public. Share and evaluate radio broadcasts in class.

• **Drama on the bridge:** In small groups, the children re-enact the moment when the iceberg is first spotted from the bridge. What do the crew believe will happen? Do they think it will be avoided? Play out the scene and share responses in a final plenary.

Extension

• **Research and presentation:** Working individually or in pairs, the children conduct further research into this extraordinary maritime story. Encourage them to make use of as many different sources of information as possible, including the Internet, CD-ROMs, books and encyclopaedias. Check out the following websites for useful information: www.bbc.co.uk/history/society_culture/society/titanic_06.html and www.titanicpark.com .

Name _____ Date _____

FULL STEAM AHEAD...

Imagine you are one of the crew members on board the Titanic.
How do you feel? What do you think the trip will be like?

Write a short conversation between you and a fellow
crew member, in which you share your hopes about the
trip ahead, and the prospect of seeing America for the
first time.

_____   _____

           _____

_____   _____

           _____

_____   _____

           _____

_____   _____

           _____

_____   _____

           _____

_____   _____

           _____

TEACHER'S NOTES

Introduction

• Load up the Mind's Eye CD-ROM. You may like to tell the children what the title of the session is before you reveal the image, or just open up the picture and watch their initial reactions to it.

• With the whole image in view, encourage the children to share their first impressions, brainstorming any key words and phrases that come into their heads as they look at the picture, e.g. *wedding, family, love, dressing up, special occasion, partners, bouquets.*

Familiarisation

• How many guests are in the picture? Who is related to whom? Invite suggestions about the roles the figures have in the extended families of the bride and groom.

• Invite the children to share their knowledge and experience of weddings. Who has been to a ceremony? What was it like? Did everything run smoothly? What were the photographs like? What part did they play in it (pageboy, bridesmaid, guest)?

Exploration

• Where, and when, do the children think this photograph may have been taken? Look closely at the clothes, the background, the haircuts, and so on, for clues. Discuss also the possible implications of this being in sepia, or black and white, rather than colour.

• What do the children think the guests are looking at? Encourage them to picture the studio in their mind's eye, and describe what they can see, looking in the direction of the camera: *photographer, flash lights, onlookers waiting to be in the next shot,* etc.

Italian immigrants in American photographer's studio, circa 1920-1930.
© Phodo / Alamy

ACTIVITIES

 Speaking

• **Hot-seating:** Ask volunteers to come to the front of the class and sit in the 'hot seat' (a free chair) and answer questions from the floor in the role of one of the guests in the photograph. Questions refer to: *what the wedding was like; how they're feeling; what they think of the bride/groom; did they enjoy the lunch?*

• **Whispering guests:** If some of the guests in the picture were to whisper to one another during this photo session, what might they say? In pairs or small groups, the children share theories and then perform their whispers to the class, e.g. *'These shoes are killing me!'; 'Can we get this over with, I'm starving!'; 'She's standing on my dress!'*

Listening

• **Reported conversations:** In pairs, the children exchange their ideas for the perfect wedding. Where would they like to be married? What would the cake be like? What about the dresses and suits? How would they arrive at/leave the wedding venue? Come together to share views, each child speaking on behalf of their partner.

Group Discussion

• **Group discussion:** Begin a class discussion in which you address the following question: *Why do we dress up for weddings? Where did the customs we have now come from? Is it necessary to have a ring, a cake, a bouquet, smart clothes and so on? Why do we do it like this?* Talk about tradition, sense of occasion, to make it a memorable day, to share good news with family, etc.

Drama

• **Still image:** Arrange the class into two or three large groups. Explain that each group must assemble themselves into a shape that replicates the gathering in the photograph. Each group member takes a role. Go around the groups, saying 'cheese' at which point the 'guests' smile/strike interesting facial expressions.

• **Thought tracking:** Using the same groups as above, each group takes a turn to reassemble in their position for the photograph while the other children watch. At a given point everyone strikes a pose and holds a facial expression while the teacher says 'cheese'. The others must guess what each guest is thinking, based on their expression and body language.

Extension

• **Research and presentation:** Ask the children to work in pairs, researching different kinds of wedding ceremonies around the world. Focus on customs, values and traditions. Share findings in a final plenary.

Name _____ Date _____

WEDDING DAY BLUES

Imagine you are either a bride or a groom on your wedding day. Your bridesmaid or best man tells you that (s)he has either a) lost the ring, b) lost the bouquet, c) dropped the cake or d) forgotten to book the cars!

Choose one of the dramas and write out a short duologue (performed conversation). How will your friend break the bad news to you? How will you react? What will happen next? How will you resolve the problem?

_____ _____

         _____

         _____

_____ _____

         _____

         _____

_____ _____

         _____

         _____

_____ _____

         _____

         _____

_____ _____

         _____

         _____

_____ _____

         _____

Now see if you can learn your words and perform your duologue to the class. Try to sound as convincing as you can!

TEACHER'S NOTES

Introduction

- Load up the Mind's Eye CD-ROM. You may like to tell the children what the title of the session is before you reveal the image, or just open up the picture and watch their initial reactions to it.

- With the whole picture in view, revisit the children's ideas and brainstorm any key words and phrases as they are encouraged to 'say what they see'.

Familiarisation

- Look closely at the image together and try to ascertain where and when this photograph may have been taken. Look at the architecture, horse as transport, clothes, road.

- Elicit the children's existing knowledge and experience of 'spaghetti westerns' and the 'Wild West'. Brainstorm any key words that we might associate with cowboy films: *saloon, pistols, cattle, ranch, duel, coach-train, gold-diggers* and so on.

Exploration

- Invite the children to decide what may be happening in this particular image. Consider, if this was a scene from a film, who is this man, and why are the two characters on the street corner staring at him? Are they old fashioned police officers or sheriffs? Do they belong in a western? Share theories and scenarios.

- Continue the discussion above to explore what might happen next. Could someone run out of the saloon door? Is this man about to meet his rival for a duel? Share ideas.

A solitary rider.
© Daniel Farson/Hulton Archive/Getty Images

ACTIVITIES

Speaking

- **Hot-seating:** Ask for volunteers to sit in the 'hot seat' (a chair at the front) and answer questions from the floor in the characters of the rider, the men on the street corner, and/or person inside the building looking out.

- **Duologues:** In pairs, the children prepare, rehearse and perform short duologues in which they pretend to be the men on the street corner, looking over at the rider. What might they be saying to one another? Share work.

Listening

- **Story narration:** In a class circle, or in smaller groups, the children improvise a collaborative story in which they each contribute a line to move the plot along. The story must be set in the place in the image, and involve the characters within it, but others may be introduced too. Start the story off with: *I arrived in a strange town and the first thing I saw was a man on horseback...*

 Group Discussion

- **Class discussion:** Focus the children's attention on the rider. Consider how transport has changed over the years. If a mysterious stranger arrived in town today, how might he travel? What would be the most impressive way of arriving in a new place today? Helicopter? Jetpack? Share ideas.

Drama

- **Group scene:** In groups of about three or four, the children set up the scene as it appears in this still image, pretending they are on a film set. Once each group has set up, the director (teacher) shouts 'Action!' and the scene is played out. What will happen next?

- **Playscript:** In writing groups, the children draft, rehearse and perform a short playscript about a stranger who rides into an old town in the 'wild west'. Who is he? Why is he here? How do the locals react when they see this visitor? Keep the playscripts to a short length and then listen to play-readings. Appraise each one together.

Extension

- **Research and presentation:** Ask the children to find out more about the history of cowboys in America. Where and when did they originate? What were their lives like? Why do they still continue to be the subject of so many films and dramas? The children may work in research groups, or individually, and then share their findings in class. The following website is an excellent resource: www.cowboyshowcase.com

Name _____ Date _____

THE LONE RANGER

Write and perform a poem about a lonely cowboy or cowgirl who rides from town to town, working on ranches and camping outside.

Think about:

- the appearance of the character
- the setting in which they ride
- where they sleep, eat and work.

Begin by brainstorming some useful key words and phrases that you could include. Here are a few – can you add some of your own?

weather-beaten face	**drinking moonshine**
sun-soaked prairies	**sleeping under the stars**

Now learn the words and perform it for your class. Perhaps you could even try an American accent!

TEACHER'S NOTES

Introduction

• Load up the Mind's Eye CD-ROM. You may like to tell the children what the title of the session is before you reveal the image, or just open up the picture and watch their initial reactions to it.

• With the whole image in view, share first impressions of the scene, recording initial observations: *windmills, corn, orange sky, fields, wind, sails.*

Familiarisation

• Brainstorm key words and phrases to capture the features, colours and moods of the picture.

• Elicit the children's prior knowledge and experience of windmills. How do they work? What are they used for? Where do we usually find windmills?

Exploration

• Look closely at the image and invite the children to imagine they are looking at the scene through the eyes of someone, or something at the scene, hiding in the long grass. Who, or what, is it? Share and record ideas on the board.

• Encourage the children to see the setting in their mind's eye: broaden the view and describe what else is there, in other directions. What would you come to if you walked left or right or behind the image?

Windmills in Holland.
© Wilmar Photography.com/Alamy

ACTIVITIES

Speaking

• **Talking pairs:** Invite the pairs to discuss, and make lists of different words they can construct using the letters: W-I-N-D-M-I-L-L. Share these in a final plenary: who has the most? Who has made the longest word?

• **Descriptive words:** Ask the children to work in small groups, or individually. They must make two lists of adjectives: one to describe the scene in the evening; the other to describe this place at dawn. Encourage them to focus on their five senses when reaching for interesting, vivid descriptions.

Listening

• **Whispers in the wind:** Divide the class into two teams. One team stands at one side of the classroom and the other stands at the opposite side. Ensure that each person has a partner opposite them. The children take turns in calling messages to their partner, while the others simulate the sound of the wind! Can they hear their partner's words? Can they repeat the message back?

Group Discussion

• **Group discussion:** Begin a class discussion on different types of power/energy sources, beginning with wind power *(water, coal, sun, oil, nuclear)*. Which do the children think is the safest/cheapest/most sustainable? Which was the most popular one hundred years ago? Which will be the most common in one hundred years time?

• **Group stories:** Ask the children to work in groups of about four or five. Sitting in a circle, they take turns to contribute a line to an improvised story set in a windmill. Their title could be 'The day the wind stopped blowing'.

Drama

• **Group movement:** In groups, the children prepare a short display in which they simulate the movement of a windmill, from the sweeps (sails) turning to the shafts, spurwheels and mill-stones inside the mill. Give each child a 'part' to play! Check out the following website for a useful diagram. www.shipleywindmill.org.uk/sec.htm

Extension

• **Research and presentation:** Divide the class into groups of about four. Each group must research one of the principal energy sources mentioned in the class discussion above. The children may use the Internet, CD-ROMs, encyclopaedias and magazines to find their information. The groups give short presentations in which they share their findings (using visual aids as far as possible).

Name _____ Date _____

TALKING – AND DRAWING – WINDMILLS! ABC

Imagine an alien has arrived at your door. He, she, or it, wants to know how we humans use the weather to help us live and work. First on their research list is 'windmills'.

Work with a partner. One of you pretends to be the alien (who luckily has learnt our language), the other must explain what a windmill is and what it does.

Remember, the explanations will have to be clear and use very simple words and phrases.

_____

_____

_____

_____

_____

_____

_____

_____

_____

_____

_____

_____

Now work out a set of instructions to enable the alien to draw the windmill without ever actually seeing one! Your instructions will need to be very clear. You are only allowed to tell them where to move their pencil across the page!

TEACHER'S NOTES

Introduction

- Play the first few seconds of the audio clip and then pause it. Invite the children to explain what could be making this sound.

- Continue to play the whole clip for the class. Discuss the children's first impressions and record any key words and phrases on the board. Encourage them to 'say what they hear' at this initial stage.

Familiarisation

- Replay the clip and establish that it is the sound of an emergency vehicle speeding through city traffic. Focus also on the sound of the voices at the very beginning, and other sounds like a motorbike speeding past.

- Elicit the children's prior knowledge and experience of emergency vehicles. List the different types of services there are. Which might this one be? How can we tell?

Exploration

- Play the clip once more and consider where this vehicle may be going, and why. What are the voices saying at the beginning of the clip? Share theories together.

- Brainstorm the first words everyone thinks of when they hear a siren like this one. Record words and phrases on the board, e.g. *fire, accident, 999, rescue team, emergency, in a hurry, help on its way.*

Audio clip
ACCIDENT SCENE (26 secs)

ACTIVITIES

Speaking

- **Hot-seating:** Invite volunteers to sit in the 'hot seat' at the front of the class and answer questions in the role of the driver of this vehicle. Where are they going? What has happened? What are they expecting to find?

- **Word tennis:** In pairs, the children volunteer to sit on two chairs at the front, opposite one another. The first player 'serves' by calling out one example of a sound you might hear in a city. The other player 'returns' with a new sound, and so on, until someone falters and loses the point. Sounds could include: *doors slamming, people chattering, planes overhead* and so on.

Listening

- **Sound effects:** Play the clip again and ask the children to focus specifically on the tone of the siren. In pairs, they try to simulate this siren noise! Can they capture the right tone, length, rhythm? Share attempts. Try other sirens, for other emergency vehicles.

- **Questions:** Explain to the children that if they were to call 999 and report an accident/crime/fire, both they and the telephone controller would need to have excellent listening skills, in order to respond to the questions put to them. What sort of questions would the controller ask? List these in pairs and share them in a plenary.

Group Discussion

- **Class discussion:** Consider together how we, as bystanders, react when we witness an accident. Do we stand and stare? Do we move on our way and leave it to the experts? Why do many of us feel a need to watch? Are we caring or just curious?

Drama

- **Group role-play:** In groups, the children act out a scene in which a family is cooking a meal in the kitchen, and chatting. Suddenly the chip pan catches fire. What do they do? What happens next? They will need to call 999 and report the fire – one member may play the part of the telephone operator. The children prepare, rehearse and perform the sketch. (You may wish to show two versions: what to do, and what not to do.)

Extension

- **Research and presentation:** Ask the children to find out more about the emergency services. Divide the class into research groups, and give each group a particular emergency service to research, finding out information like: a typical day, range of emergencies attended, qualifications needed, etc. Examples could include: *lifeboat, mountain rescue, police, fire, ambulance, breakdown.*

JOB VACANCY

Prepare a short radio advertisement in which new recruits are sought for a branch of the emergency services. It may be police, fire, ambulance, mountain or sea rescue.

You will need to think about:

- the type of work carried out
- qualifications required
- rates of pay
- the sort of character needed.

Learn the words of your script and perform it for the class. Remember to make the job sound exciting!

_____

_____

_____

_____

_____

_____

_____

_____

_____

_____

TEACHER'S NOTES

Introduction

- Play the first second or two of the audio clip for the children. Elicit their first reactions to the sound. What could be making this noise?

- Continue playing the trip to the end. Then revisit the children's initial impressions. Encourage them to 'say what they hear' and compile key words and phrases on the board, i.e. *talking, laughing, shouting, moaning* etc.

Familiarisation

- Try to establish together whether the people talking in the clip are young or old, male or female. How can we tell? Is this a class of school children? How old are they?

- Elicit the children's ideas about where this sound clip may have been recorded. Encourage them to think beyond the idea of a classroom and look for other possibilities, e.g. *changing room, dining hall, youth centre, stadium* etc.

Exploration

- Explore words and phrases together that accurately capture the atmosphere in the room on the clip. (*chaotic, lively, friendly, rowdy, casual, informal, noisy*). Then consider together how these sounds make the children feel. Words might include: *anxious, tired, excited, relaxed, nervous*, depending on whether they are talking and joking in a group, or listening to others' noise!

- Explore what might be happening in the clip: are these children waiting for a teacher to arrive? Or are they arguing amongst themselves? Might they be waiting outside somewhere, in a queue? Put suggestions on a mind-map on the board.

Audio clip
SCHOOLS – ARGUMENTS (58 secs)

ACTIVITIES

Speaking

- **Hot-seating:** Invite volunteers to sit in the 'hot-seat' at the front of the class and answer questions in the role of one of the children in the audio clip. Can they explain where they are, and what they are doing?

- **Talking at once:** Consider together what happens when we all talk at once. Can we understand each other? Why do we need to have some sort of order or system for talking in class, e.g. raising a hand, passing the shell around etc? Try simulating the sounds on the clip by getting everyone to talk at the same time (just for a few seconds!). Then share feedback.

Listening

- **Chinese whispers:** Explain that sometimes when we talk to one another, our words are misheard. At other times we might even be misquoted by others – such is the process of 'Chinese whispers'. In a circle, practise sending round a message and see if it has changed by the time it reaches you again!

Group Discussion

- **Class discussion:** What is the best environment for our classrooms? Do we work better in silence or when we talk to one another, or a bit of both? What sort of classroom do the children prefer? Share ideas and opinions.

- **Class discussion:** Ask the class: *Have you ever sat at a dinner table with someone who talks too loudly? Have you ever been in a restaurant when a diner at another table has a very loud voice?* Share experiences and discuss the importance of table manners! Think of the school's own lunch arrangements when discussing this.

Drama

- **Group role-play:** In groups, the children act out a scene in which a class is waiting for a teacher to arrive in the classroom. Some in the class think they should go and get help/inform a teacher that they are alone, while others in the group enjoy the freedom while they can. What will happen? How will it be resolved? Perform the scenes and then discuss what the children should do in such circumstances.

Extension

- **Discussion and brainstorm:** In groups, the children consider together how we all communicate. What are the different ways of getting your thoughts across? List the different forms of communication on the board, beginning with: *talk, facial expression; body language; sign language, mime, writing words down* etc.

Name _____ Date _____

CLASSROOM RULES

In a small group, discuss the classroom rules you currently have. Are they followed by everyone? Do they work?

In your group, come up with 10 new classroom rules that create a happy and safe experience for all of you to enjoy!

After you have discussed your ideas together, write down your 10 rules below. Try to be positive! You could begin with,

Together we promise to:

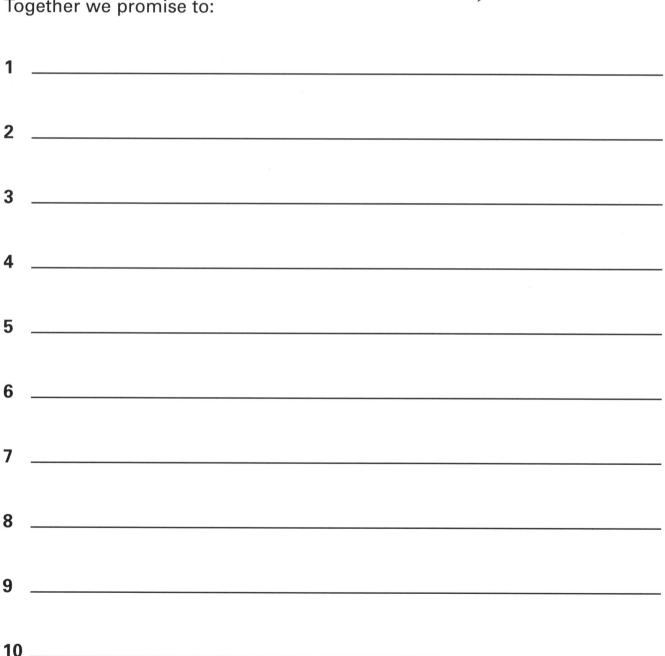

1 _____

2 _____

3 _____

4 _____

5 _____

6 _____

7 _____

8 _____

9 _____

10 _____

TEACHER'S NOTES

Introduction

• Play the first few seconds of the audio clip and then pause to elicit the children's reactions to the sound. What could be making it? Do they recognise the sound?

• Play the whole clip to the end and then revisit the children's first impressions. Is it what they expected?

Familiarisation

• Establish that this is, of course, the sound of a very appreciative audience. Invite the children to share their knowledge and experience of being in an audience. Where might one hear this sort of applause? List answers on the board, such as *theatre, cinema, music concert, comedy show*. Remind the children that this sound may equally be the welcoming of a special VIP guest, e.g. the Queen.

• Discuss why we clap to show our appreciation. What a strange tradition! What could we do instead? Good answers could include; *beat our chests, stamp feet, wave our arms about, click our fingers.*

Exploration

• Replay the clip and explore together why this particular audience might be clapping. Are there any clues in the clip to suggest where they are, such as *interior acoustics, small audience rather than a large one,* etc?

• Explore together what might happen next in the clip. Would we hear the sound of someone performing an encore? Or would we hear people talking and moving about as the audience leave? Discuss the word 'encore'. What does it mean? Where does it come from? (French for 'more'.)

Audio clip
CROWD APPLAUSE (17 secs)

ACTIVITIES

Speaking

• **Talking pairs:** In pairs, the children compile a list of the different ways we show our appreciation as an audience, e.g. *whistling, shouting 'encore' or 'more', clapping, stamping our feet, standing out of respect.*

Listening

• **Circle game:** Explain to the class that you are about to call out numbers on a scale between 1 and 5. They are acting as an audience, and the number 1 means they are unimpressed (hissing and booing) and at the other end of the scale, 5 means they are overjoyed. Call out numbers in a random order and the children must react, with their voices, body language and facial expressions.

 Group Discussion

• **Class debate:** Why do we need to have theatres with television and DVDs around? Do we need to see live drama? Debate the following motion in class: *This House believes that theatres are the best way of appreciating drama. They must never be replaced by cinemas.* The children exchange views and listen sensitively to one another's opinions.

• **Group discussion:** In groups, the children discuss what impresses them, as a member of an audience. What would make them clap and shout for more? Do they like music concerts, dances, comedians, impressionists, serious drama or farces? Share responses in a class plenary and record the most popular attractions overall.

Drama

• **Group tableaux:** In groups of four or five, the children set up the closing scene of a theatre performance of some kind. Wait for the players strike their final positions 'on stage' and then play the sound clip of the crowd applauding. The players must slowly relax, come together, hold hands and bow neatly. How will they acknowledge the applause? A slight nod of the head and a smile? How important is it to remain modest?

Extension

• **Research and discussion:** In pairs, or working individually, the children find out more about the history and tradition of theatre in this country and around the world. Where did it originate? Using the Internet, CD-ROMs and books, the pupils compile information and share it in a final plenary.

Name _____ Date _____

MIXED FEELINGS...

Imagine you and a friend are leaving the theatre after watching a play together. One of you absolutely loved the show but the other did not enjoy it at all and has very different feelings about it.

How will your conversation flow? Will you agree to disagree? Which aspects of the show will you like or dislike?

Think about:

- the cast
- the scenery and props
- the sound and lighting
- the music.

Write your conversation as a short script below. Learn your words and perform it for your class.

_____

_____

_____

_____

_____

_____

_____

_____

_____

_____

Mind's Eye/Speaking & Listening Year 5/CROWD APPLAUSE

TEACHER'S NOTES

Introduction

- Play the entire clip, which is only three seconds long. Take the children's first impressions as they 'say what they hear', i.e. a groan/wince/moan/cry in pain.

- Establish that this is the sound of someone wincing in pain. Is it a man or a woman, young or old? How can we tell?

Familiarisation

- Elicit the children's knowledge and experience of suffering a minor injury. How did they react? Why do we feel the need to use our voices when we hurt ourselves? Is it a release of tension / frustration? Is it to attract others' attention and sympathy? Or is it simply an automatic response? Encourage the class to share their opinions.

- How could we express what this person is saying in actual words? Replay the clip and invite the children to put what this person says into words, e.g. *'huh, ooh, aagh!'*

Exploration

- What do the children think might have happened here? Why is this person crying out in pain? Or is he performing a special karate move? The children share theories about what has caused this person to make such a noise.

- How else can we capture cries of pain in words? How do characters react to pain in a story? Explore words and phrases together that accurately reflect the pain or frustration someone feels when they hurt themselves (avoid swear words!), for example, *ouch!, aagh!, ooh!, youch!, oof!, aw!, oh!.*

Audio clip
MALE OW (03 secs)

ACTIVITIES

Speaking

- **Hot-seating:** Take turns to sit in the hot seat at the front of the class and answer questions in the role of the person on the audio clip. The children ask: *How did you hurt yourself? Did it surprise you? What lessons have you learned from the experience?*

- **Circle game:** Seat the class in a large circle around you. Take turns to let out a cry of pain. Each time the person must make a new noise, not one already heard. They may invent a new sound, when the more obvious ones have been used up. Have some fun with it!

Listening

- **Reported conversation:** In pairs the children interview one another about a time when they hurt themselves unexpectedly. How did they feel? Did they let out a cry of pain? What did they say? Did they gain any sympathy from others around them or just laughter? Report back to the class, the children speaking on behalf of their partners.

 Group Discussion

- **Class discussion:** Replay the clip once again and consider how it makes you feel. Do the children find it humorous? If so, why? Consider why we often find other people's mishaps funny. Shouldn't we feel sympathy instead? Share stories when we have chuckled because someone has fallen over, perhaps on stage or in a film, and assess why we laughed. Discuss the importance of offering sympathy/understanding when it happens in real life.

Drama

- **Slow motion scenes:** In pairs, the children prepare, rehearse and perform a short scene in which they act out a slow motion fight scene. Encourage them to show their facial expressions in slow motion too – and any cries of pain to accompany them. Share in class and evaluate. Remember to stress to the children that stage-fights such as these require a great deal of careful planning and thought!

- **Sound effects:** In pairs, the children prepare, rehearse and perform a mime in which one person is very accident prone, and the other provides all the sound effects, including the knocks, bangs and exclamations.

⊘ Extension

- **Group plays:** In writing groups, the children write a sketch in which a person suffers a minor accident in front of passers by. What will others do? They will need to react differently: some chuckling, others ignoring, others providing assistance and comfort. The children write the play together and then perform it for the class.

CLUMSY CLOWNS

Write your own poem about a person who is very clumsy.

You will need to think about:

- what happens to them
- the words they use
- the facial expressions they show
- the reactions of others around them.

You could begin each line with a different exclamation and then say what they have done, for example: 'Ouch! I've stubbed my toe!'

Draft your poem in rough and then copy it into the space below.

TEACHER'S NOTES

Introduction

- Play the clip and then pause it after a second or two. Elicit the children's initial responses to the sound. Invite guesses about who, or what, might be making this noise. Record the children's ideas on the board.

- Continue the clip to the end. Revisit the children's initial thoughts. Is this what they were expecting? Encourage the children to put what they hear into proper words, e.g. *growl, roar, shuffling, rustling*.

Familiarisation

- Elicit the children's theories about what this sound actually is. Establish together that it is the sound of a lion growling and shuffling about in a cage.

- Elicit the children's knowledge and experience about big cats generally, and lions specifically. Has anyone seen a lion close up? Where? What did it feel like to be so close to the 'king of the jungle'?

Exploration

- Consider together why this lion might be growling? Where could he be located? Do the children think he is angry/frustrated/hungry? How do animals express their feelings? How can we tell when a lion is upset? Share thoughts together in class.

- Play the audio clip once again. Ask the children to consider the following thought: if this was not a lion, or any sort of animal, what could it be? List ideas on the board, e.g. *thunder, someone with terrible indigestion* and so on!

Audio clip
LION GROWLS (32 secs)

ACTIVITIES

Speaking

- **Preferences:** In groups, the children discuss and compile a list of favourite jungle animals, each child expressing their preference, with reasons. At the end, share group feedback and compile a chart of favourite animals. Will the lion come out on top?

- **20 questions:** In pairs, the children take turns to think of a zoo animal and then invite their partner to ask a series of 20 questions to ascertain what the animal is, the answers to which may only be 'yes' or 'no'.

Listening

- **Listening game:** Seat the class in a large circle around you. Distribute roles as jungle animals around the class in pairs, with two of each animal. The identical animals must be sitting opposite one another across the circle. Begin improvising a quick story to describe a safari you have been on. Whenever you mention an animal, the pairs must stand up and race around the circle to see who reaches their place first.

Group Discussion

- **Group brainstorm:** Divide the class into groups of about three or four. Give the groups a set time limit (one minute perhaps) to list as many different big cats as they can think of. Share lists at the end, including *lion, tiger, black panther, puma, leopard, cheetah.* You can repeat the exercise with other species, e.g. apes.

- **Class debate:** Consider the following motion: *This House believes that the tiger should be crowned king of the jungle. It's time for the lion to step down.* Encourage the children to prepare short speeches in support, or opposing the motion.

Drama

- **Hot-seating:** Invite the children to take turns to sit in the 'hot seat' at the front of the class in the role of a jungle animal of some sort. The issue to be discussed is 'Who should be made king of the jungle?' The animals must give their own preferences, supporting their choices with reasons.

Extension

- **Research and presentation:** Divide the class into research groups of about four. Give each group a type of big cat to research. Encourage the children to use any means possible to find out more about their particular big cat, and then to prepare a group presentation for the class. Share and evaluate the group's work and then discuss how well each group worked together.

LION ON THE LOOSE!

Imagine a lion has escaped from a city zoo. Your task is to write a news report to appear on television, announcing that the lion has escaped and warning local residents to be on their guard.

Write your report as a playscript. You will need to include a newsreader, a reporter at the scene, and one or two eyewitnesses.

Begin drafting your playscript in the space below and continue on a separate sheet if necessary.

_____

_____

_____

_____

_____

_____

_____

_____

_____

_____

TEACHER'S NOTES

Introduction

- Play the first moment of the audio clip and then pause it. Invite the children to share their initial reactions to the sound. Exchange theories about what might be making this noise.

- Continue to play the clip to the end, then revisit the children's first impressions. Were they correct?

Familiarisation

- Establish that this is obviously someone laughing. Is it a man, woman, boy or girl? How can we tell?

- Elicit the children's knowledge and experience of how (and why) people laugh. Share different laughs in class! Do the children know people with strange laughs? Can they emulate them for the class to hear?

Exploration

- Replay the clip and ask the children to consider why this person may be laughing. What has set him off? Record the children's different theories on the board, e.g., *a joke, someone falling over, having an accident, making a mistake, a misunderstanding.*

- Ask the class to imagine that this person is laughing at a very inappropriate moment, when he should have been serious! Explore possible scenarios and list them on the board. Examples could include: *performing a surgical operation, meeting the Queen!*

Audio clip
MALE LAUGHTER (03 secs)

ACTIVITIES

🗣 Speaking

- **Telling jokes:** In pairs, the children tell each other jokes. Ask them to prepare, rehearse and perform them for the class. They could begin with the words, *I say, I say, I say… .*

- **Circle game:** In a large circle, explain to the children that years ago when the king went to bed, the courtiers in his palace would have to remain silent. So, the footman would go upstairs, stand outside the king's chambers and listen for the snores. He would then return downstairs and announce to the servants: *Ladies and Gentlemen, the King has gone to bed.* The children must now repeat this line, whilst pretending to carry a candle-holder. As they say 'bed' they must blow out the candle and do all this without laughing, or risk sitting out. Keep repeating until few children are standing!

👂 Listening

- **Laughter game:** Explain to the class that you will be calling out numbers on a scale of 1 to 5, where 1 represents a chuckle, and 5 is a belly laugh. The children change their laughter accordingly as you call out different numbers. Identify and share notable performances.

👁 Group Discussion

- **Class discussion:** Consider together the questions: *What makes us laugh? Why do we do it? Can we actually help it?* The children exchange views, listening and responding to others' opinions. Invite the children to share stories of when they have had a fit of giggles when they shouldn't have done!

🎭 Drama

- **Role-plays:** In groups, or in pairs, the children revisit the situations discussed earlier in which people might suffer an attack of the giggles at an inappropriate time. Each group chooses one such time and plans, rehearses and performs a short sketch around it. Share performances in class.

❗ Extension

- **Stories:** The children write, and read out, excerpts from imaginary stories in which a person suffers an attack of giggles at the wrong time. They will need to describe in detail the serious circumstances in which it happens and the reactions of those around the character when they see him/her laughing. (A Prime Minister's speech might be a good one to choose!)

Name _____   Date _____

BE SERIOUS PLEASE!

With a partner act out a scene in which you are both expected to be serious, but one of you is unable to stop laughing. You might choose: a police interrogation, a parent's evening, or perhaps a marriage proposal!

Introduce the scene using stage directions and then write what you might say in the space below. Remember to show, in brackets, who is supposed to be laughing, and when.

_____

_____

_____

_____

_____

_____

_____

_____

_____

_____

_____

Now learn your words and perform your scene to the class.

Mind's Eye/Speaking & Listening   Year 5/MALE LAUGHTER

TEACHER'S NOTES

Introduction

- Play the first few seconds of the audio clip and then pause to elicit the children's first reactions to the sound. What do they think could be making this sound?

- Play the clip to the end and then revisit the children's initial impressions. Welcome suggestions from the class about where and when the clip may have been recorded.

Familiarisation

- Establish that this is the sound of an open air market during the daytime. Play the clip once again and this time listen out for recognisable words and phrases. Ask the children to share what they can hear, e.g. *'pure wool – for a single bed, not a double'*.

- Share knowledge and experience of markets in a class discussion. Who has visited an open air market like this one? Can the children describe the atmosphere when they were there? Did they enjoy their visit? Did they buy anything?

Exploration

- Explore words and phrases together that accurately capture the atmosphere of such a market, e.g. *loud, chaotic, cheerful, friendly, busy, prosperous* etc.

- Play the clip once again and explore together the sorts of merchandise one might find for sale at such a market, such as *household goods, fruit and vegetables, tools*.

Audio clip
MARKET ATMOSPHERE (19 secs)

ACTIVITIES

 Speaking

- **Sales talk:** In pairs, the children practise their sales patter! Can they repeat the words and phrases they heard on the clip? Can they invent some of their own phrases that might 'reel in' a customer to buy their goods? What will they sell? How will they attract the attention of passers by? Share performances in a plenary session and evaluate how persuasive they sound.

- **Brainstorm:** In pairs again, and using a large sheet of paper for writing on, the children brainstorm all the words and phrases they can think of that are associated with selling, buying and bargaining, such as: *two for a pound; roll up, roll up; I won't say ten – I won't even say five!*

Listening

- **Circle game:** In a circle, invite the children to take turns reciting the following line: *I went to the market today and I bought... .* Each person adds an item to the list, but not before remembering all those that have gone before. You may extend this to include prices for each item as well, e.g. *a tea-towel for 50p, a pair of gloves for £2.00* and so on.

 Group Discussion

- **Class discussion:** Consider together the following questions: Do we still use markets regularly? Are they less popular nowadays? What may have replaced them in some towns? What does an open air market offer that a supermarket does not? Some examples include: *personal service, amusement, cheap bargains, variety, heritage and tradition, sense of community.*

Drama

- **Role-play:** In pairs, the children act out scenes in which a market stall holder seeks to persuade a customer to buy his/her wares. Refer the children back to the phrases brainstormed in the Speaking section above.

- **Rain stops play:** In large groups, or as a whole class, the children act out scenes in which a market is suddenly hit by stormy weather. Stalls are blown around, goods are soaked, and the customers all run for cover. Encourage the children to show the moment the storms hit through their body language and facial expression (this could be an effective mime).

Extension

- **Planning committee:** Divide the class into groups of about four or five. Each group acts as a planning committee for a new market that is due to come to town on a Saturday morning. The local council has granted them space for 10 market stalls. Which goods will they sell? They must decide which stallholders will be welcomed for the first week, so make a list of the goods they regard as essential and/or likely to make the most money.

Name _____   Date _____

NEW MARKET IN TOWN

Design an eye-catching poster to advertise a new street market that is coming to your town. The poster will be put in shop windows and on notice boards.

You will need to think about:

- the venue
- times of opening
- types of goods on sale
- facilities such as food and drinks available.

Draft your poster in the space below, then copy it onto a large sheet of paper.

TEACHER'S NOTES

Introduction

• Play the first few seconds of the audio clip and then pause to elicit the children's first reactions to the sound. What could be making it? Could it be an animal of some kind? Or a machine?

• Continue to play the whole clip and then revisit the children's responses. Are they any clearer now? Brainstorm key words and phrases on the board as the children are encouraged to 'say what they hear'. Good examples are: *screech, scrape, thud, groan, knock, grating.*

Familiarisation

• Replay the clip and then consider if anyone has heard a similar sound before. Invite the children to share stories of places they have been, or things they have heard that may be similar to the sounds on the audio clip.

• Compile a shortlist of words and phrases that sum up what this sound could be. Focus particularly on the echoing quality of the sound. Is this the interior of somewhere? Perhaps it is a steel ship, submarine, spaceship docking at a space station, or perhaps even a robotic whale beneath the sea.

Exploration

• If this is the sound of a vast ocean liner, ask the children to describe what it might look like and record key words and phrases on the board, for example: *rusty, heavy, cumbersome, industrial, echoing interior* and so on.

• Consider together the sorts of feelings this sound clip evokes. How do the children feel when they hear it? Are these sounds lively and upbeat, or slow and sluggish? Share ideas and responses, and record any key words and phrases on the board, e.g. *melancholy, sad, depressed, thoughtful, reflective, unhappy, miserable, tired.*

Audio clip
METALLIC SOUND (23 secs)

ACTIVITIES

Speaking

• **Talking pairs:** Working in pairs, the children decide on a particular theory about what is making this sound, and then try to convince the others in the class to agree with them. They will need to listen carefully to the clip and support their comments with evidence. Vote on the most popular theory.

• **Sound simulators:** Replay the clip once again and divide the class into pairs. Invite each pair to see if they can simulate the sounds on the clip using nothing but their own voices. Share attempts in class.

Listening

• **Circle game:** Seat the class in a circle. Take turns to call out the names of different sounds, e.g. *hum, buzz, splash, screech, skid, tinkle* etc. If anyone repeats a word, or hesitates by saying 'erm' they must sit out! Remind the children that many of these words are termed 'onomatopoeic' (words whose sound and meaning are the same).

Group Discussion

• **Group discussion:** What sounds do vehicles make? In groups, the children discuss and then write down as many different sounds as they can, putting them in pairs with their vehicles, for example: *train/rattle, bicycle/ clatter* or *squeak; helicopter/whirr.* Share at the end. Which group has the most sounds? Do some vehicles make similar sounds?

Drama

• **Group role-play:** In groups, the children act out a scene that makes sense of the sounds on the clip by using the audio clip as a sound track to their scene. Scenarios could include: *working on a submarine; exploring an old, disused oil tanker; fishing for whales.*

• **Alien attack!:** In groups again, the children prepare, rehearse and perform a scene in which the sound effects are coming from an alien spaceship that lands on Earth. How will the humans react to their visitors? Are these sounds the aliens' way of communicating with us? Complete the scene.

Extension

• **Research and discussion:** Explain to the children that the sounds in the clip sound quite metallic (from metals). In research groups, the children find out more about different types of metals. Which metals are used to make ocean liners, submarines and space rockets? Share findings in a class discussion. List the different metals, and their uses, on the board.

DID YOU HEAR THAT?

Imagine you are exploring an old ship with a friend. Suddenly you hear a series of strange noises, like the ones in the clip. What are they? What is happening to the ship? Is there someone – or something – after you, or is the ship actually trying to talk?

Write the script for your scene below. Learn your words and perform it for the class. Remember to use lots of expression to bring the end of the story to life.

_____

_____

_____

_____

_____

_____

_____

_____

_____

_____

TEACHER'S NOTES

Introduction

• Play the clip and then pause it after a second or two. Elicit the children's initial responses to the sound. Invite guesses about who, or what, might be making this noise.

• Continue to play the whole clip for the class and then revisit the children's first impressions. Was this what they were expecting? Establish that this is the sound of someone eating loudly!

Familiarisation

• Elicit the children's experience of noisy eaters. How does it feel to be dining with one? Is this regarded as bad manners? Share stories and thoughts around the class.

• Discuss the children's ideas about who this person might be: is it a man or woman, or an old or young person? Play the clip again and try to identify together what this person is saying ('oh, great, yeah, it's really nice!').

Exploration

• What do the children think this person might be eating? How can they tell?

• Explore other ways we might react to a food that we a) like, and b) dislike strongly. Record key words and phrases on the board: e.g. *delicious, yummy, heavenly, sweet, tasty* or *sour, bitter, unpleasant, gross!*

Audio clip
MALE SILLY EATING (13 secs)

ACTIVITIES

Speaking

• **Noisy eaters!:** Ask the children to re-enact the audio clip themselves, by simulating the sounds and words of the person they hear. Share performances in class and judge who is the best scoffer!

• **Talking pairs:** In pairs, invite the children to make a list of words and phrases that act as synonyms for the word 'eating', e.g. *scoffing, munching, feasting, gorging, cramming.* Share these words in a final plenary, recording them on the board for all to see. Do they all mean the same thing, or are there subtle differences between them?

Listening

• **Reported conversation:** In pairs once again, the children discuss their favourite and least favourite foods. In a class plenary, invite feedback and then compile a list of top favourite foods and the least favourite ones too!

 Group Discussion

• **Class discussion:** Why/how do we actually taste food? What do our taste buds actually do for us? What does it mean to taste? Do we taste things differently from each other? How can we tell if our senses of taste are all the same? Can two people try the same food but come away with different taste sensations?

• **Group discussion:** How do animals eat their food? Brainstorm key animals and the way they eat their prey/food. Some good starting points are: *lions tear, birds peck, cats lap and a snake swallows whole!*

Drama

• **Role-play duologues:** In pairs, the children prepare, rehearse and perform a scene in which one person eats very loudly and the other becomes irritated. Eventually the latter turns to the noisy eater and tells him/her to quieten down and have some manners!

Extension

• **Research and presentation:** In research groups of about three, the children find out more about traditional dishes we associate with different countries around the world. They will need to compile a list as they go, retrieving information from books, atlases, CD-ROMs and the Internet. Share feedback in a final plenary, in which the pairs present their findings. Then ask which of these foods have become part of our vocabulary and culture today. You might display your information on a world map, drawing or writing the food on it.

Name _____   Date _____

Write your own set of table manners that might appear outside your school dining hall, for everyone to pay attention to. Remember, the aim of good manners is to enable other diners to enjoy their meals too, in peace and quiet!

On a separate sheet of paper, make a poster that sets out your new rules, with illustrations.

_____

_____

_____

_____

_____

_____

_____

_____

_____

_____

_____

_____

TEACHER'S NOTES

Introduction

- Play the first few seconds of the audio clip and then pause to elicit the children's first reactions to the sound. What could be making it? Do they recognise this sound?

- Play the whole clip to the end and then revisit the children's first impressions. Ask them to 'say what they hear' in the clip and record key words and phrases on the board, e.g. *gurgle, bubble, slosh, drops, drips* etc.

Familiarisation

- Elicit the children's prior knowledge and experience of water and the way it ripples and moves about. Replay the clip. Where have they seen water rippling and sloshing in this way and heard such sounds? List on the board, beginning with: *bath, swimming pool, the sea, pond, Jacuzzi.*

- Play the clip once again and try to identify what is happening to move the water around in this way? For example, *paddling, arms bathing, swimming, wading.*

Exploration

- Focus now on what is happening in this specific clip. What is the most popular theory, (refer to the ideas in the Familiarisation above)?

- Could this sound be outside? How can we tell? Listen again to the clip and discuss the differences between interior acoustics. Broaden the discussion to consider how loud swimming pools tend to be. Why is that?

Audio clip
WATER SOUNDS (12 secs)

ACTIVITIES

🗣 Speaking

- **Hot-seating:** Invite volunteers to come up to the 'hot seat' at the front of the class (teacher's chair) and take questions from the floor in the role of the person who is actually making the sound in the clip. What is (s)he doing? Swimming? Bathing? You might say that the person cannot give the answer, but the others must guess it in 20 questions, the answer to which may only be 'yes' or 'no'.

- **Talking pairs:** In pairs, the children consider the following question: *If you could only have a bath or a shower fitted in your home, which would you have and why?* Consider the options: baths can be a great way to relax, unwind, soothe those aching muscles, but a shower gives you a refreshing burst in the morning, or a cooling down in the summer! Share thoughts.

👂 Listening

- **Circle game:** In a large circle, take turns to say one word we associate with water (e.g. *splash, gurgle, bubble* etc). No one is allowed to repeat a word that has gone before, and hesitation is also prohibited!

👁 Group Discussion

- **Group discussion:** In small groups, the children brainstorm key words and phrases together to sum up how people feel when they take a bath at the end of a very long and tiring day. Words could include: *relaxed, peaceful, stress-free, calm, serene.* Then consider how we feel during a shower: *refreshed, cool, revitalised, energised.*

🎭 Drama

- **Solo performances:** Individually the children find space in the classroom/hall/playground. Invite them to mime a short scene in which they are trying to summon up the courage to step into a very cold swimming pool! How will they do it? Will they ease in gradually, toe first, or will they plunge in and bear it? Encourage the children to emphasise those facial expressions!

- **Group role-play:** In groups, the children pretend they are paddling through the sea on holiday together, when suddenly one of them makes an amazing discovery. Is it treasure? Or perhaps some gold? Or a message in a bottle? What happens next? Share performances in class.

ⓘ Extension

- **Advertisement:** In groups, the children write, rehearse and perform a short radio or television advertisement for a company that sells hot tubs, or Jacuzzis. The children will need to focus on how these products can help customers to rid the stress from their lives and feel refreshed and revitalised! Share performances and evaluate which advertisement was the most persuasive and why.

Name _____   Date _____

Working with a partner, design a poster to inform young swimmers how to keep safe when they visit the seaside and swim in the sea.

Your advice may include:

- always stay in shallow water where you can stand up
- stay in sight of an adult at all times
- never try to surf waves without a surf board
- try to keep your mouth closed and breathe through your nose
- if the water looks and feels polluted, get straight out!

Draft your poster in the space below and then copy it out neatly onto a large sheet of paper.

OPPORTUNITIES FOR CROSS-CURRICULAR LINKS TO QCA SCHEMES OF WORK (DfES Standards Site) in Mind's Eye Y5

Mind's Eye Y5 Unit IMAGES 1-20	Cross-curricular links (QCA Schemes of work)
ABSEILING	**Science:** Unit 3F Light and shadows; **Geography:** Unit 15 The mountain environment; **ICT:** Unit 6A Multimedia presentation
AIR TRAFFIC CONTROL	**ICT:** Unit 2E Questions and answers; **Citizenship:** Unit 01 Taking part; **Geography:** Unit 18 Connecting ourselves to the world
ASTRONAUT	**Science:** Unit 5E Earth, Sun and Moon; **Citizenship:** Unit 11 In the media – what's the news?
AURORA BOREALIS	**Science:** Unit 5C Gases around us, Unit 3F Light and shadows; **Geography:** Unit 7 Weather around the world
CAVE RESCUE	**Geography:** Unit 19 How and where do we spend our time? **ICT:** Unit 2C Finding information
CHARIOT	**History:** Unit 18 What was it like to live here in the past?; Unit 6A Roman case study; **D&T:** Unit 2A Vehicles
CLOCKS	**Citizenship:** Unit 02 Choices; **D&T:** Unit 2C Winding up
EGYPTIAN TUNNEL	**History:** Unit 10 What can we find out about ancient Egypt from what has survived?
HELP THIS WAY	**Citizenship:** Unit 04 People who help us, Unit 02 Choices
LONDON EYE	**Geography:** Unit 8 Improving the environment, Unit 16 What's in the news?; Unit 21 How can we improve the area we see from our window?; **D&T:** Unit 6C Fairground
MACHU PICCHU	**History:** Unit 16 How can we find out about the Indus Valley civilisation?, Unit 1 What were homes like a long time ago?; **Geography:** Unit 15 The mountain environment
ORANG-UTAN	**Citizenship:** Unit 03 Animals and us; **ICT:** Unit 2C Finding information
SKYDIVING	**Geography:** Unit 19 How and where do we spend our time?; **Science:** Unit 6E Forces in action
SPACE STATION	**Science:** Unit 5E Earth, Sun and Moon; **Geography:** Unit 16 What's in the news?; **Citizenship:** Unit 02 Choices
SPOOKY MANSION	**History:** Unit 1 What were homes like a long time ago?
THE BLITZ	**History:** Unit 9 What was it like for children in the Second World War?; **Citizenship:** Unit 02 Choices
TITANIC	**ICT:** Unit 2C Finding information, Unit 4D Collecting and presenting information
WEDDING	**RE:** Unit 1D Beliefs and practice; **Citizenship:** Unit 05 Living in a diverse world
WILD WEST	**Citizenship:** Unit 01 Taking part, Unit 02 Choices; **ICT:** Unit 2C Finding information
WINDMILLS	**Geography:** Unit 8 Improving the environment

Mind's Eye Y5 Unit SOUNDS 1-10	Cross-curricular links (QCA Schemes of work)
ACCIDENT SCENE	**Citizenship:** Unit 02 Choices, Unit 04 People who help us; **Geography:** Unit 12 Should the high street be closed to traffic?
CLASSROOM	**Citizenship:** Unit 02 Choices; Unit 08 How do rules and laws affect me?
CROWD APPLAUSE	**ICT:** Unit 2C Finding information; **Geography:** Unit 19 How and where do we spend out time?
CRY IN PAIN	**Citizenship:** Unit 01 Taking part, Unit 02 Choices
LION GROWLING	**Science:** Unit 4B Habitats, **Citizenship:** Unit 03 Animals and us
MALE LAUGHTER	**Citizenship:** Unit 01 Taking part
MARKET ATMOSPHERE	**Geography:** Unit 12 Should the high street be closed to traffic?, Unit 19 How and where do we spend out time?
METALLIC SOUND	**Science:** Unit 3C Characteristics of materials; **Music:** Unit 2 Sounds interesting – Exploring sounds
SCOFFING FOOD	**Science:** Unit 3A Teeth and eating, Unit 5A Keeping healthy; **Citizenship:** Unit 02 Choices; **ICT:** Unit 4D Collecting and presenting information
WATER SOUNDS	**ICT:** Unit 6A Multimedia presentation; **Science:** Unit 4D Solids, liquids and how they can be separated; **Geography:** Unit 11 Water